Wall Street, Trade, and the New Economy

Volume II

The Rise of Finance

Copyright © 2016 by Neville Buck Marshall

All rights reserved
Printed in the United States of America
First Edition

For information about permission to reproduce selections from this book, write to SWIFT Act Alliance, 1900 W Chandler Blvd, STE 15-285, Chandler, AZ 85224.
Email: info@swiftact.com

Cover design by Shon Quannie
Website: www.4x-media.com

ISBN: 978-1530560912

Library of Congress Control Number: 2016904560
CreateSpace Independent Publishing Platform, North Charleston, SC

Volume II - Contents

Preface
    The Wall Street Economy   i

Organization   1

Section

III   **The Impact of Ideas**   5
    9   New Economy Facts & Figures   7
    10   Logic of the New Economy   18
    11   Wall Street Rules   28
    12   Boom and Bust Banking   54

Quotes on Banks   64

Summary   65

Volume III - Preview
    Trade Deficits and Offshoring   67

SWIFT Act - Preview
    Smart Growth   69
    Wage Standards   69
    Industrial Policy   70
    Financial Reform   70
    Trade and Tax Reform   71

Notes   72

Appendix
    Managing the Economy   77
    Contractive Policy   78
    Expansive Policy   80
    Counter-cyclical Policy   82

Figures and Illustrations

New Economy Facts and Figures
    Figure 1: Oil Prices and Inflation   8
    Figure 2: Corporate After-Tax Profits   9
    Figure 3: Averange Family Income Growth   10
    Figure 4: Cumulative Change in Real Wages   10
    Figure 5: Productivity and Wages   11
    Figure 6: Wage Share of Productivity   11
    Figure 7: Wages and Salaries – Share of GDP   11
    Figure 8: Impact of Slow Growth – Lost Value   12
    Figure 9: Excess Financial Growth   13
    Figure 10: 2015 GDP - Financial and Real   14
    Figure 11: Real GDP Growth and Job Growth   15

Logic of the New Economy
    Figure 12: Unemployment and Inflation   22

Wall Street Rules
    Figure 13: U.S. Pension Plan Benefits   46

Appendix
    Figure A-1: Contractive Policy   78
    Figure A-2: Expansive Policy   80

The Wall Street Economy

Casino capitalism is the end result of a long term process, in which manufacturing has declined and the financial sector has expanded.

It began with financial deregulation that spawned the takeover movement.

In the 1980s, junk bonds were used to finance takeovers, in which borrowed money was used to buy companies.

Using junk bonds, corporate raiders could borrow *97 percent of the money* needed to buy a majority of company stock.

Corporate divisions and subsidiaries were then restructured into *separate companies with their own stock*, and sold off for enormous profits.

The combined stock value of divisions sold separately was far greater than the single company stock targeted for takeover.

Between 1979 and 1989, there were more than 17,000 such takeovers.

The takeover movement *forced companies to downsize*, because a smaller workforce raised the financial value of operations.

In highly profitable companies, workers were laid off because *downsizing made those companies more valuable, in terms of stock prices.*

Corporate boards also began granting stock options to CEOs, paying them to promote high prices for company stock.

The impact transformed American industry, by giving financial interests leverage over productive lines of business.

Thus, the decline of American industry financed the rise in stock values, as corporate restructuring was used to create high prices for company shares.

Beginning in the mid-1990s, *asset inflation policy* drove the telecom and dot.com booms, which collapsed in the early 2000s.

Thereafter, *asset inflation* policy drove the housing boom, intentionally created by Fed chair Alan Greenspan, which collapsed in the 2008 financial crisis.

The Fed has continued to buy toxic mortgages from Wall Street banks, *at the rate of $75 billion a month in 2013, followed by an additional $30 billion a month in 2014.*

Investing that amount of money in manufacturing would have transformed the economy.

Instead, the Fed serves the Wall Street economy, by promoting *asset inflation* in stock and house prices, instead of promoting manufacturing and the revival of American industry.

Organization

In 2011 the Occupy Wall Street movement was joined by tens of thousands of protesters in this country, and then by hundreds of thousands throughout Europe and around the world.

While Occupy was politically left of center, it was non-partisan in its criticism of Wall Street ties to the Obama administration and the Democratic Party.

The movement reflected anti-Wall Street sentiment that isn't represented in either political party, as well as opposition to free trade, which also suffers from bipartisan lack of representation.

I was struck by similarities with the anti-NAFTA campaign of Ross Perot, who won nearly 20 million votes in the 1992 election.

In the aftermath of the 2008 financial crisis, the economy fell into the worst recession since the Great Depression of the 1930s.

All too often, the cause of the Great Recession is explained in financial terms, like the role played by derivatives in collapse of the housing market.

In reality that financial complexity was only the tip of the iceberg.

While for most of us the financial story sounds like Greek, the more important story behind it is seldom told.

My writing this book is an effort to tell that story in a way that gives you a handle on what has happened to the economy.

Organization is shown for all six sections in the series. This volume covers only section three.

I: Fundamentals
Section 1 explains the dynamics of two models that show how economies grow, and how they stagnate.

These simple models can be used to compare different aspects of the economy at different points in time, and are referred to throughout the series.

Section 1 also provides an overview of today's New Economy and explains how it differs from the model of growth and why it doesn't work.

II: Background
Section 2 covers historical background that illustrates the fundamental principles outlined in the models of growth and stagnation.

Economic fundamentals in the period leading to the Great Depression of the 1930s were the same as those that led to the 2008 financial crisis.

Understanding those underlying similarities is essential to preventing a repeat of the Great Depression.

Policies implemented in this country in the 1930s, and adopted in Europe and Japan after World War II, brought long term growth accompanied by financial stability, low unemployment, and low inflation.

We need a clear understanding of what happened to disrupt that growth, and what it would take today to have it re-established.

Stagnation in the 1970s was defined by high levels of unemployment that coincided with high inflation in the same period.

From the mid-1960s through the early 1970s, presidents Johnson and Nixon pursued expansive economic policy that proved inflationary.

There were also crop failures in 1970 that drove up the price of commodities before the rise in oil prices.

Then in 1973 the price of oil tripled, which dramatically raised the cost of goods produced in manufacturing.

In 1974, price controls that had been imposed by President Nixon were lifted, so that pent up demand was also a factor contributing to inflation.

Thereafter, the price of oil doubled again between April 1979 and April 1980.

While these developments provided the context for inflation, by the late 1970s the focus had shifted to the idea that growth in wages was the root cause of inflation.

That juncture was the origin of policy that created the New Economy, which was and has remained fully bipartisan.

III: The Impact of Ideas
Section 3 outlines the impact of *anti-inflation policy* that emerged in the late 1970s, and continued through the mid-1990s.

Once full employment came to be seen as inflationary, official policy came to embrace slower rates of growth that were considered non-inflationary.

Slow growth and artificially high levels of unemployment have had serious long term consequences for the economy.

While overall growth has been slower, the composition of that growth has changed to reflect the growth of finance instead of production, and job growth in services instead of manufacturing.

Section 3 also explains the shift from *anti-inflation policy* to support for asset bubbles in the stock and housing markets.

This *asset inflation policy* drove the housing bubble, intentionally created by Federal Reserve chair Alan Greenspan, which collapsed in the 2008 financial crisis.

IV: Globalism and Decline
Section 4 explains the way the U.S. economy operates within the world economy.

The way the balance of payments system works
- U.S. trade deficits are matched by inflows of foreign capital, and
- those inflows of foreign capital are used to finance deficits in the federal budget

But the way the balance of payments system works isn't a partisan issue.

When there's no conflict between the political parties, the media treats the issue as though it isn't news worthy.

This leads to under-reporting, leaving the public unaware of a critical flaw in how the New Economy operates.

Along the same lines, globalization of production through supply chains has fundamentally changed the meaning of trade.

Trade in finished products between countries has been replaced, *by trade in components* among production centers around the world.

The result is that both the value added in production and the jobs created by manufacturing have been moved out of the country.

Reporting on the issue is muted, because there's no conflict between the political parties when it comes to trade.

This bipartisan consensus on unrestricted trade has left the U.S. economy stripped of productive capacity and unable to create jobs.

V: The Wall Street/Trade Complex
Section 5 traces the rise of global finance that occurred in tandem with the globalization of production.

In the 1990s an excess of international lending drove booms in Mexico and throughout Asia that ultimately collapsed.

The response from the U.S. Treasury department was to orchestrate bailouts of Western banks through international loan agreements.

Those bailouts were based on loan guarantees and currency devaluation for the countries involved.

The result was acceleration of offshoring and unprecedented growth of the U.S. trade deficit, driven by imports from low wage countries.

Wall Street influence in the Treasury Department has done lasting damage to the U.S. economy, in both Democratic and Republican administrations.

Section 5 also provides a case study on China's strategic trade policy, which includes a range of incentives for U.S. multinationals to offshore production.

The case study on China also includes discussion of child labor and the number of children with industrial occupations throughout Asia.

VI: End Game

Section 6 evaluates the impact of the New Economy and the consequences of continuing political support that serves to perpetuate its contradictions.

Between 1998 and 2010 the U.S. trade deficit with low wage countries brought the loss of more than 23 million jobs.

The response to this unprecedented job loss was bipartisan rhetoric about reliance in the New Economy on services instead of manufacturing.

The reality is that service sector jobs are even more susceptible to offshoring than are jobs in manufacturing.

Princeton economist Alan Blinder, a former vice chairman of the Federal Reserve, estimates between 30 million and 40 million jobs in this country are susceptible to offshoring.

Meanwhile leading figures in both political parties speak of a New Economy, based on innovation and new jobs in the service sector.

The reality is that offshoring drives the destruction of American industry and disintegration of the U.S. economy.

Section 6 concludes with discussion of the bailout function of the federal government.

The risk of financial collapse poses an even greater threat to the economy today than in 2008.

The largest banks are now much larger, while unregulated trading in derivatives is backed by federal deposit insurance.

When the next Wall Street crisis requires government bailout, the losses involved will bankrupt the Treasury.

Conclusion: Mandate for Reform

Bipartisan consensus continues to support unregulated finance and unrestricted trade with low wage countries.

The consequences have been devastating.

Financial speculation has become far more profitable than productive investment, both domestically and all over the world.

At the same time, the pattern of world development creates too little demand to support markets for American goods.

The result has been distorted development of the world economy.

The U.S. economy has been both a driver and a victim of this development, and is now at risk of irreversible decline.

SWIFT Act is a collection of proposals to restructure the economy and reverse the damage done by Wall Street influence through money in politics.

The Rise of Finance

See the appendix for discussion of expansive and contractive policy

The Impact of Ideas

In the period following World War II, the circle of growth became the blueprint for shared understanding among the industrial democracies.

But there was a different assessment for poor countries, in which growth was based on exports and alliances with multinational companies.

This double standard undermined world demand, by preventing the development of consumer markets in poor countries.

Following decades of prosperity, the post war consensus began to unravel in the 1970s.

The shock of high oil prices drove the cost of manufactured goods higher, limiting demand for American products.

The result was high unemployment and high inflation, which set the stage for reversal of policy and ideas about the economy.

The origins of the New Economy can be traced to *anti-inflation* policy of the late 1970s and early 1980s.

Comprehensive deregulation bills enacted during the Carter administration were intended to allow for cost cutting, to reduce inflation.

High interest rates imposed in 1979 and maintained in the early 1980s were designed to reduce inflation, by creating downward pressure on wages.

Then between 1980 and 1986, the price of oil fell by 71 percent, while the rate of inflation fell by 70 percent.

Yet despite the obvious impact of oil prices on inflation, the Federal Reserve continued to treat full employment and wage growth as inflationary.

In pursuit of *anti-inflation* policy, the Fed continued to use high interest rates to maintain artificially high levels of unemployment.

Long after the threat of high inflation had passed, this *anti-inflation* policy served to protect financial interests, at the cost of stagnant wages and a slowdown in overall growth.

It seems that no attention was paid to sources of inflation that had nothing to do with the fundamentals of the circle of growth.

For example, the Johnson administration's economic policy sparked inflation in the late 1960s.

Expansive policy (deficit spending and lower taxes) also continued in the Nixon administration that followed.

In the early 1970s, crop failures drove up prices of commodity imports, which also contributed to inflation before the rise in oil prices.

Thereafter, the price of oil rose three fold in 1973, and later doubled again between April 1979 and April 1980.

Yet despite these developments, policy makers continued to view wage growth as the fundamental driver of inflation.

The Federal Reserve's *anti-inflation policy* brought a dramatic change in the view of economic dynamics that define the circle of stagnation.

Instead of a problem to be overcome, *slow growth became the goal of official policy*, because slow growth was justified as being "non-inflationary" growth.

The economic impact was in line with that predicted in the circle of stagnation.

The use of profits to re-invest in production or to raise wages declined.

Instead, excess profits drove financial speculation, while the lack of wage growth undermined demand.

In the New Economy, slow growth in demand is offset by cheap imports and easy credit.

In place of higher wages, credit and long term debt have been used to maintain consumption.

As a result, the economy has been transformed by a process of *financialization*, in which financial expansion has become the primary source of growth.

Between 1950 and 1980, the share of GDP accounted for by the financial sector rose from less than 2 percent to nearly 5 percent in 1980.

Since 1980, finance has grown at more than twice the average rate for the previous thirty years.

A study by the Harvard Business School concluded this unprecedented growth of finance serves no useful purpose to the larger economy.

While excess financial profits have been used for speculation, since the mid-1980s the economy has accumulated a deficit in productive investment of $4.6 trillion dollars.

Since the 1970s, slow and distorted growth has cost the economy $15 trillion dollars in lost production.

The economy has been stripped of productive capacity, and can no longer attract the investment needed to create jobs.

The lack of wage growth has led to stagnant demand, unemployment, falling investment, and still lower demand.

Ultimately, deregulation and anti-inflation policy created the basis for financial speculation and the dysfunctional dynamics of stagnation.

Main Points

The origins of the New Economy can be traced to *anti-inflation* policy of the late 1970s and early 1980s.

Comprehensive deregulation bills enacted during the Carter administration were intended to allow for cost cutting, to reduce inflation.

High interest rates imposed in 1979 brought high unemployment, and were designed to reduce inflation by creating downward pressure on wages.

These measures coincided with a dramatic fall in the price of oil in the early 1980s.

Between 1980 and 1986, the price of oil fell by 71 percent, while the rate of inflation fell by 70 percent.

Thereafter, the continued pursuit of *anti-inflation* policy (long after the threat of inflation had passed) created long term trends that transformed the economy.

Trends:

Corporate after-tax profits % of GDP
- 1963 – 2003: 5.7%
- 2004 – 2010: 8.8%
- 2011 – 2014: 10.1%

Net business investment % of GDP
- 1960 – 1984: 4.0%
- 2005 – 2014: 2.1%

Wages as share of GDP
- 1947 – 1974: 51.5%
- 2005 – 2014: 43.2%

Real growth rate of GDP
- 1875 – 1972: 3.4%
- 1974 – 1993: 2.9%
- 1994 – 2015: 2.5%
- 2012 – 2015: 2.0%

Job Growth as ratio to GDP growth
- 1970s – 8.1%
- 2000s – 1.2%
- 2011 – 2014: 2.8%

New Economy Facts and Figures

In the early 1980s deregulation progressed in tandem with the Reagan platform to reduce spending and cut taxes.

Reagan also wanted to maintain the high interest rates imposed by the Fed in the last year of the Carter administration.

Federal Reserve chairman Paul Volcker, a Carter appointee, was retained by Reagan despite opposition within the Republican party.

Volcker initiated a tight money policy by raising interest rates to historically high levels.

Under Volcker the fed funds rate (rate at which banks lend to one another) was raised in 1979 and then in the early 1980s to more than 19 percent.

Despite the ensuing recession and high unemployment, the policy played a critical role in defeating inflation.

From a high of over 13.5 percent in 1980, inflation fell to 3.2 percent in 1983, a decline of 70 percent.

At the same time, between 1980 and 1986 the price of oil declined by more than 71 percent.

After adjusting for inflation, by the end of Reagan's term oil prices had fallen well below the 1974 average.

Prices remained low thereafter, with the inflation adjusted average in the late-1990s still only 23 percent of what it had been in 1980.

Paul Craig Roberts argues that the Reagan tax cuts brought about the decline of inflation.

In an environment of high inflation, Supply side theory argues that lower taxes allow demand to drive an increase in output, instead of causing inflation.

Roberts has pointed out that while Volcker began raising interest rates in 1979, there was no corresponding fall of inflation.

Even so, the extremely rapid decline of inflation from 13.5 percent in 1980 to 3.2 percent in 1983 seems far too sudden to be attributed to the impact of lower taxes.

Moreover, the 1981 tax cut was followed by a substantial increase the following year, as well as by numerous subsequent increases throughout Reagan's term.

Bruce Bartlett estimates roughly half the 1981 tax cuts were reversed through later increases during Reagan's eight years in office.

Whatever the impact of high interest rates might otherwise have been, the policy was reinforced by the market after oil prices peaked in 1980, falling 36 percent by 1983 and 45 percent by 1985.

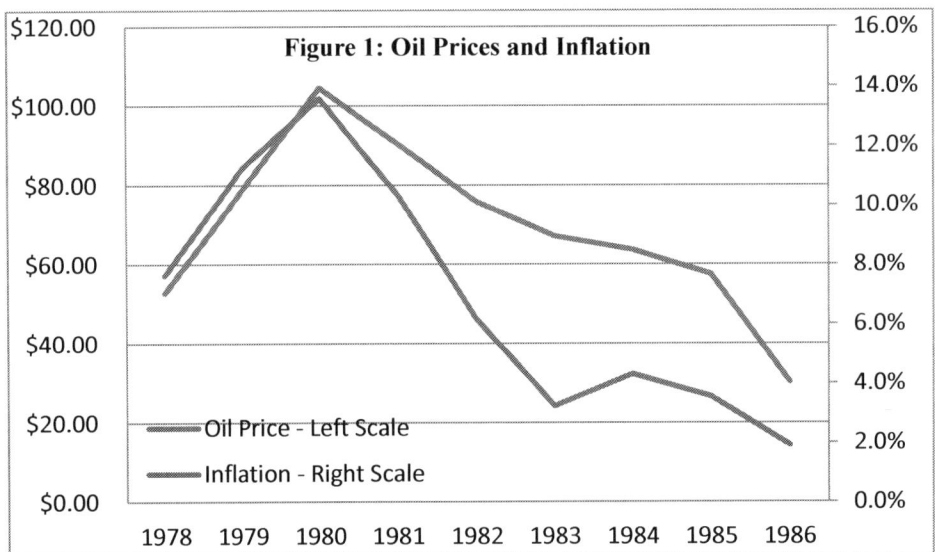

Source: Inflation rate from Bureau of Labor Statistics. Oil prices from inflationdata.com (accessed 4/15/2014: comparison in 2014 dollars)

In inflation adjusted dollars, the price of oil fell from $104.49 per barrel in 1980 to $30.26 in 1986, a decline of 71 percent.

As shown in Figure 1, between 1980 and 1986 the oil price fell by 71 percent, while the rate of inflation fell by 70 percent.

While there will always be debate over the impact of Reagan's policies, public memory seems lacking when it comes to the impact of falling oil prices on inflation.

High interest rates were effective in overcoming inflation *in the context of falling oil prices*.

Volcker's tight money policy, which in fact was precisely what Keynes would have recommended, has long been correctly understood as appropriate in the context of inflation.

Even so, the rapid decline of inflation in a very short period was also clearly a function of the fall in oil prices that occurred at the same time high interest rates were implemented.

Like the impact of falling oil prices on inflation, the importance of context is also clearly evident in the logic of deregulation.

The 1970s stagnation was a period in which inflation spiraled out of control.

Unions tried to limit the erosion of wages by indexing wages and other benefits to inflation, which only made the problem worse.

More damaging still was the impact on public attitudes toward unions.

Despite high oil prices, the public ultimately laid the blame for inflation on unions and blue collar wages.

Politically, Carter embodied the shift with his deregulation of transportation industries and his agreement with Volcker to use high interest rates to induce recession.

Both men understood that inducing recession would amount to using high unemployment to overcome inflation.

Reagan followed suit in his decision to keep Volcker as chairman of the Federal Reserve, and in his breakup of the air traffic controllers strike in 1981.

The union had refused to back Carter and endorsed Reagan during the presidential campaign. But the air traffic controllers union was a government union, making the strike illegal.

Reagan ultimately fired 11,345 controllers who refused to return to work, in a move considered a watershed for the union movement.

Union membership in the private sector was 28 percent in 1976 but declined under Carter to 20.6 percent in 1980, and declined further under Reagan to 12.9 percent in 1988.

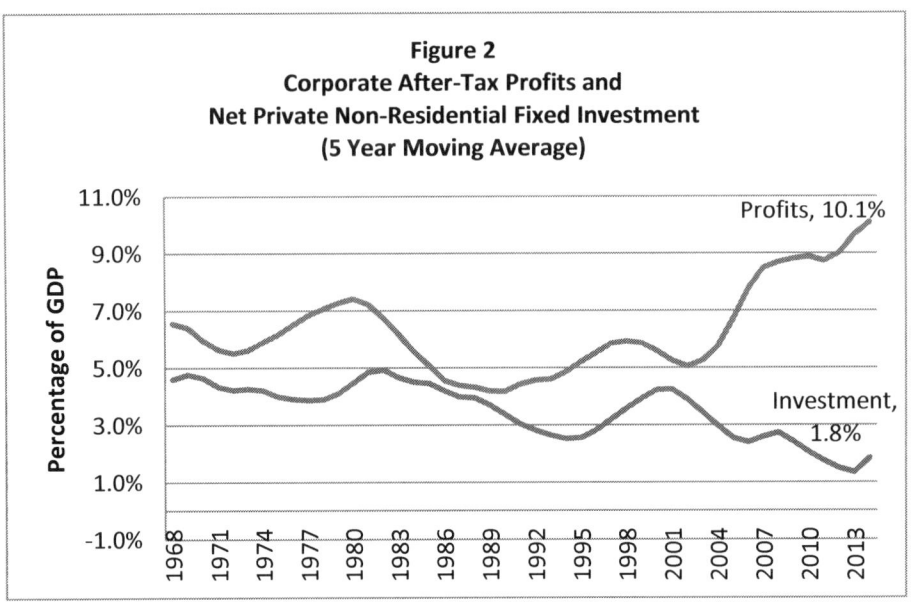
Source: Bureau of Economic Analysis.

In a public opinion survey at the time, 51 percent of respondents supported Reagan's breakup of the strike.

In a span of only 12 years, private sector union membership declined by more than 50 percent.

By 2000 the rate had fallen to 9 percent, and in 2010 was just 6.9 percent, the lowest rate for private sector employees in over a century.

As union membership has declined, wages have stagnated.

While inflation dropped with the dramatic fall in oil prices in the 1980s, median wages today, adjusted for inflation, are barely higher than they were in 1973.

Finally, between 1985 and 1987 the dollar was devalued by 50 percent relative to the Japanese yen and German mark, which spurred U.S. exports and supported gradual recovery thereafter.

Deregulation and the decline of unions kept wages from rising, while the dollar devaluation helped exports and drove the rebound in profits.

Figure 2 shows corporate after tax profits, which rose under Carter until Volcker imposed high interest rates in 1979.

After the recession that followed, profits rose from a low of 3.1 percent in 1986 to 4.9 percent in 1988 to an average 5.1 percent in the early 1990s.

Corporate profits continued to rise thereafter, and before the financial crisis reached the highest level on record in 2006.

Corporate profits today are more than 60 percent higher than the average rate of the 1950s.

In the same period corporate profits were rising, business investment was declining.

From 1960 to 1984 the average net private non-residential investment was 4 percent of GDP.

Compared to the historic rate of 4 percent, net private non-residential investment has declined, to an average 2.1 percent of GDP since 2005

In this context of low investment, a number of long term trends since the late 1970s reflect an uncanny consistency.

These trends go beyond fluctuations that can be attributed to business cycles, or to differences between Republican and Democratic administrations.

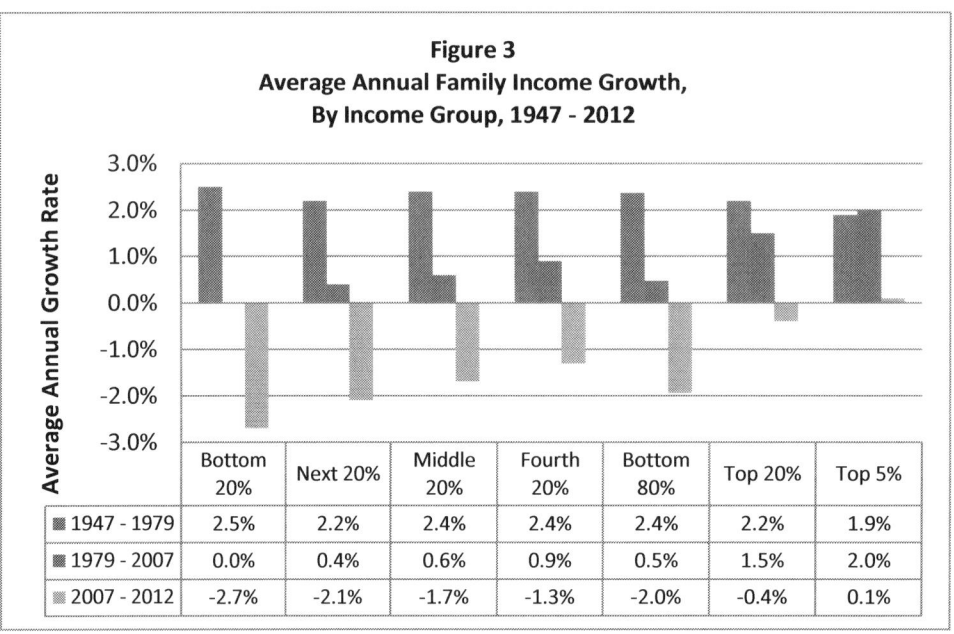

Source: Elise Gould (2014). Why America's Workers Need Faster Wage Growth--And What We Can Do About It. (Washington, D.C.: Economic Policy Institute), Briefing Paper #382, page 9.

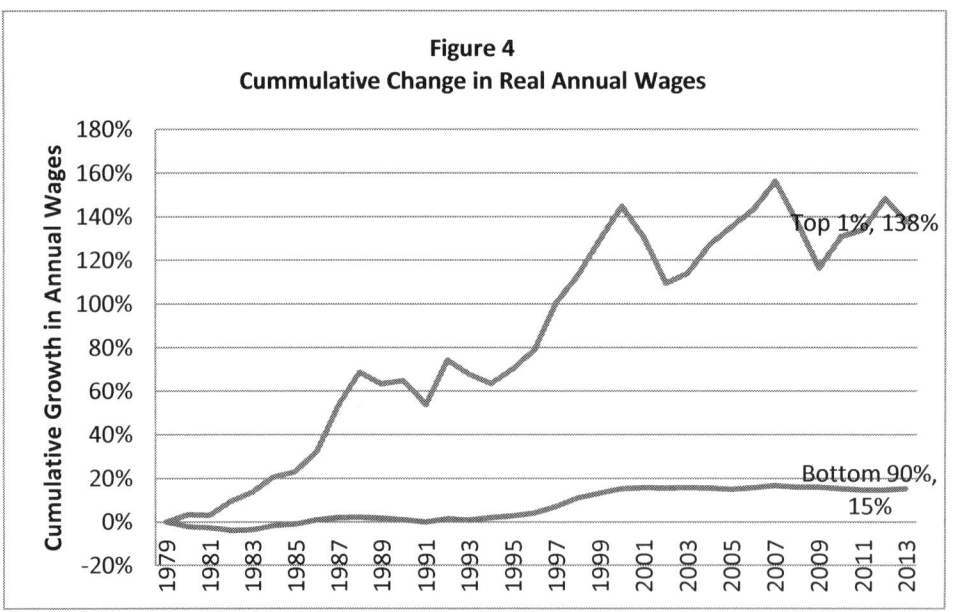

Source: Lawrence Mishel, Elise Gould, and Josh Bivens (2015). Charting Wage Stagnation in Nine Charts. (Washington, D.C.: Economic Policy Institute). EPI analysis of data from Kopczuk, Saez, and Song (2010) and Social Security Administration wage statistics. Reproduced from Figure F in Raising America's Pay: Why It's Our Central Economic Policy Challenge.

Rising Inequality

Consider the issue of inequality that was highlighted by the Occupy Wall Street movement, and more recently by politicians from both parties.

Figure 3 shows annual *family income growth* from 1947 through 2012, broken down by family income group.

Between 1947 and 1979, for the bottom 80 percent of families, average annual income growth was 2.375 percent.

In the period between 1979 and 2007, for the bottom 80 percent of families, average annual income growth was 0.475 percent (less than half of one percent).

That change in the rate of income growth represents a decline of 80 percent.

Note that in the period between 1947 and 1979, the economy was based on manufacturing.

But in the period between 1979 and 2007, the economy was gutted by the loss of manufacturing through offshoring.

Over nearly 30 years, annual income growth, for the bottom 80 percent of families, grew at a rate that was 80 percent slower than the average rate in the 30 years prior to 1979.

This dramatic change took place before the Wall Street financial crisis of 2008.

Figure 4 shows annual income growth *by wage group.*

Between 1979 and 2006, income growth for the top one tenth of one percent (0.01%) was **20 times faster** *than that of the bottom 90% of wage earners.*

If income growth had continued unchanged from the average rate for 1947 – 1979, median household income in 2007 would have been higher by nearly $18,000 dollars.

Yet even this magnitude of difference for *household* income ignores the fact that women only began entering the workforce in large numbers in the 1970s.

The fact is, prior to the 1970s household income was based on one income.

In 2007 median household income was nearly $18,000 lower than it would have been if the growth rates of 1947-1979 had continued, despite the prevalence today of two income households.

Inequality is also more than simply an issue of fairness.

Low income families spend by far the largest proportion of their incomes on consumption.

So while the economy depends on consumption, the pattern of growth for more than 30 years has resulted in a decreasing share of income for those who spend the most on consumption.

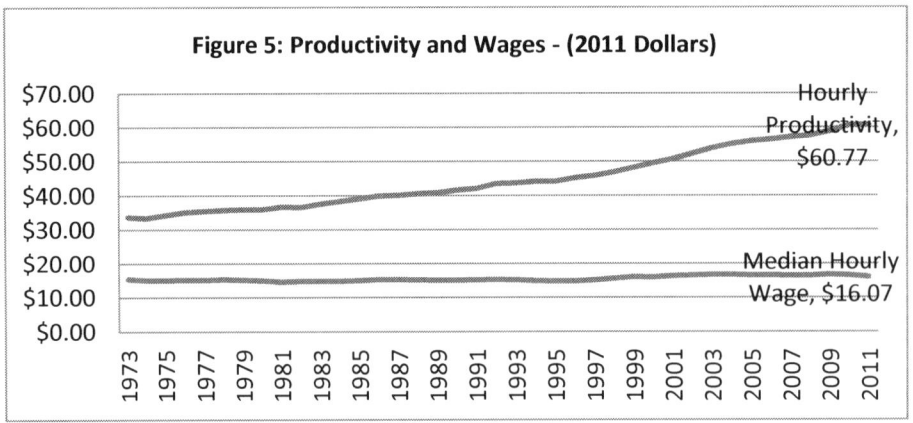

Source: Lawrence Mishel, and Kar-Fai Gee, "Why Aren't Workers Benefitting from Labor Productivity Growth in the United States?," International Productivity Monitor, No. 23, Spring 2012, page 38 and appendix tables compiled by the Economic Policy Institute.

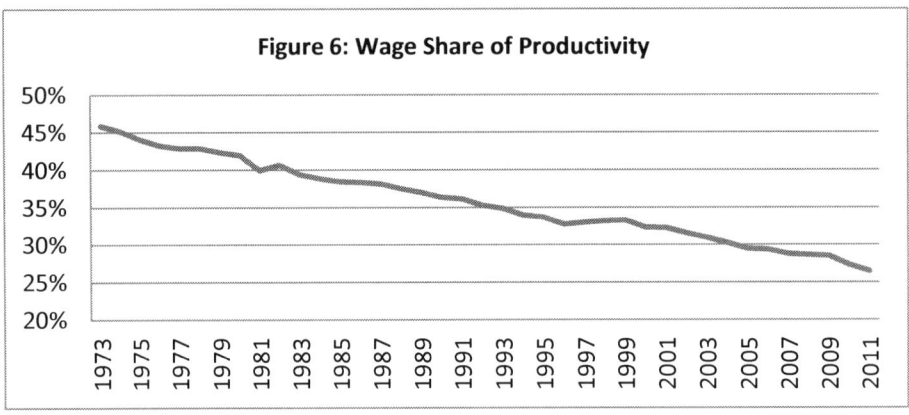

Source: Same as figure 5.

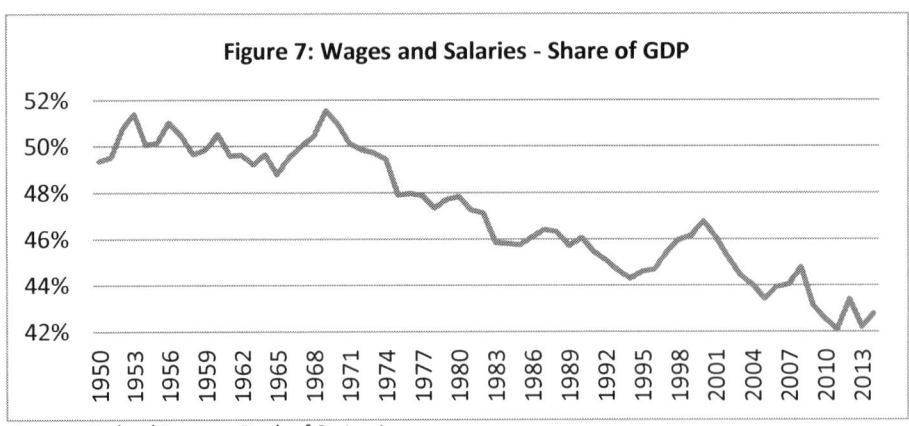

Source: Federal Reserve Bank of St. Louis.

While the pattern is counter-productive for generating demand, it has also grown progressively worse and been thoroughly bipartisan since the Carter administration.

Decoupling Productivity and Wages
The source of growing inequality can be found in the progressive decoupling of productivity and wages.

Figure 5 shows the value of an hour of work and the median hourly wage, in 2011 dollars.

In 2011 dollars, an hour of work in 1973 created $33.68 of value, while the median hourly wage was $15.45.

In 2011 the value of an hour of work had risen to $60.77, while the median hourly wage was only $16.07.

Adjusted for inflation, the median hourly wage rose by 1.6 cents a year, while hourly productivity rose by 71 cents a year.

Figure 6 shows the declining wage share in percentage terms.

The wage share of productivity fell from 45.9 percent in 1973 to only 26.4 percent in 2011, a decline of some 53 percent.

Clearly, one source of the rise in corporate profits is this dramatic fall in the share of productivity paid in wages.

Despite the large scale entry of women into the workforce, *household income has declined because the wage share of value created from work is less than half what it was in 1973.*

This lower wage share is the source of excess profits, which have been diverted to
- foreign investment in low wage countries, and
- financial investments that have little impact on employment.

Again, the decline has been both persistent over a long period and fully bipartisan.

Figure 7 shows the proportion of wages and salaries in the economy, referred to as the wage share of GDP.

In the 28 years between 1947 and 1974, annual wages and salaries averaged 51.5 percent of GDP.

The wage share of GDP fell below 50 percent in 1974 and has been declining ever since, averaging 43 percent since 2005.

The difference between the historic average and the recent average rate is 8 percent of GDP.

In 2014, 8 percent of GDP amounted to $1.3 trillion dollars.

Today *annual* wages from employment are $1.3 trillion less than they would be if the proportion of wage income in the economy was at 1973 levels.

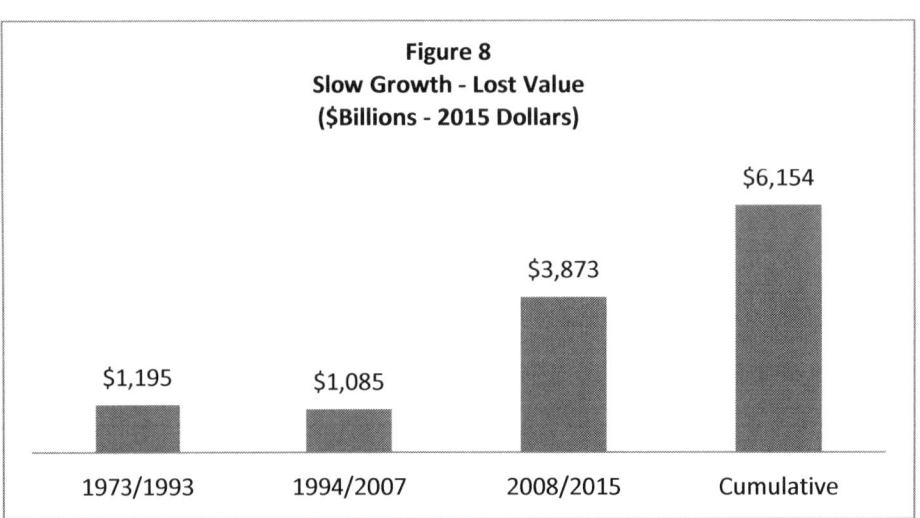

Source: Economic Research Service, USDA (2012). Real Historical Gross Domestic Product (GDP) and Growth Rates of GDP for Basline Countries/Regions. Based on World Bank World Development Indicators, International Financial Statistics of the IMF, IHS Global Insight, and Oxford Economic Forecasting, as well as estimated values developed by the Economic Research Service. Author's calculation of difference between 3.4% historic average rate of growth and growth rates cited.

Well over $1.3 trillion dollars that is not being paid through *annual* wages and salaries is contributing to corporate profits, *but is also not being allocated to productive investment.*

Slow and Distorted Growth
The third trend since the 1970s has been a decline in the overall rate of GDP growth, coupled with changes that reflect much more rapid growth of the financial sector.

Between 1870 and 1973, the U.S. economy grew at an average annual rate, including the period of the Great Depression, of 3.4 percent.

That was the inflation adjusted average rate of growth from the period after the civil war, spanning more than a century of our economic development.

Between 1973 and 1993, the average rate of growth fell to 2.9 percent.

That decline of 0.6 percent means the economy was growing at a rate *nearly 13 percent slower* than the historic average rate of growth.

Then between 1993 and 2016, the average rate of growth fell to a little less than 2.5 percent.

Over the past 20 years, the economy has been growing 26 percent more slowly than the historic average.

Finally, in the four years between 2012 and 2016, the average rate of growth fell to just 2 percent.

Two percent annual growth is more than 40 percent slower than the historic average.

Official statements aside, the economy can't generate enough jobs at the current rate of growth.

In 2015, eight years after the onset of recession, the economy grew at an annual rate of only 2 percent.

In this book I rely on official figures, which may well understate the economic damage caused by slower growth overall.

Using the government's own data, Figure 8 shows the economic damage done by slow growth since 1973.

As of year-end 2015, slow growth has created a cumulative loss of more than $6.1 trillion in production value.

While decline in the rate of overall growth has been costly, the composition of growth has also been distorted by rapid growth of the financial sector.

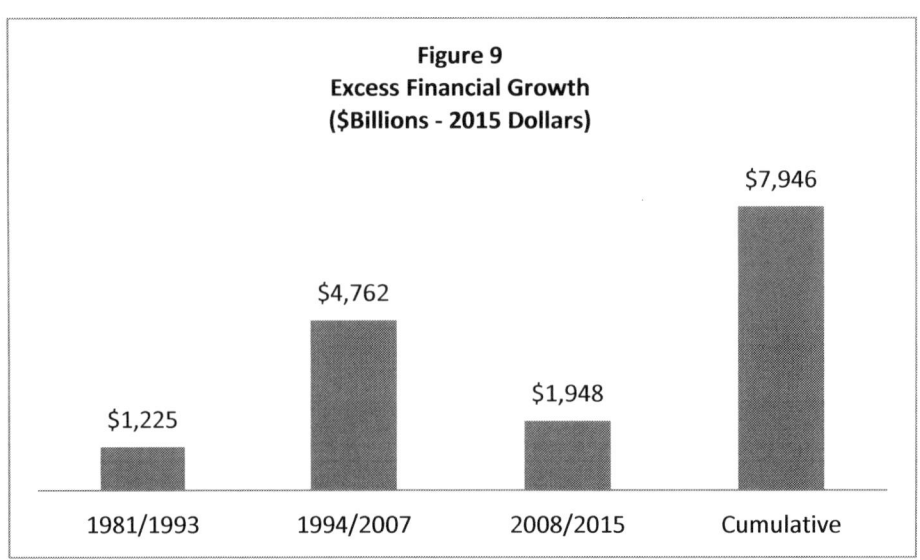

Source: Bureau of Economic Analysis. Author's calculation using 1980 baseline of 4.9% value added in GDP by Financial sector.

Harvard Business School professors David Scharfstein and Robin Greenwood have tracked the rate of financial sector growth over more than 60 years.

The financial industry accounted for 2.8 percent of value added in GDP in 1950, and rose to 4.9 percent in 1980.

Since 1980, the average growth rate for the financial sector was almost double the rate in the thirty years before.

Scharfstein and Greenwood argue there is no reason the financial sector should have become less efficient in today's economy, as measured by the rising cost to other economic sectors.

Figure 9 shows the value of excess growth in the financial sector.

By 2015, excess financial sector growth, over and above the 1980 baseline, had reached a cumulative value of nearly $8 trillion dollars.

Excess financial growth of $8 trillion means that same value was not accounted for by industrial growth.

This change in the composition of growth is a measure of the New Economy, marked by consumer debt and the decline of manufacturing.

Although minor by comparison, another source of excess financial profit has been oil speculation.

After rising substantially in 2004, oil prices continued rising through 2013.

In 2011, ExxonMobil CEO Rex Tillerson testified before Congress that 40 percent of the oil price was accounted for by speculation.

The New York Times reported one estimate that speculation cost the U.S. economy $200 billion dollars a year.

The source of speculation has been special exemptions granted by the Federal Reserve, and relaxed regulations approved by Congress, that allow Wall Street banks to own non-financial businesses.

The banks now own infrastructure that includes pipelines, refineries, and fleets of oil tankers, as well as companies that control operations at major ports.

In addition to speculation in oil prices, the New York Times also reported on the role Wall Street has played in driving up the price of aluminum and other commodities.

**Figure 10
2015 GDP - Financial and Real
($Billions - 2015 Dollars)**

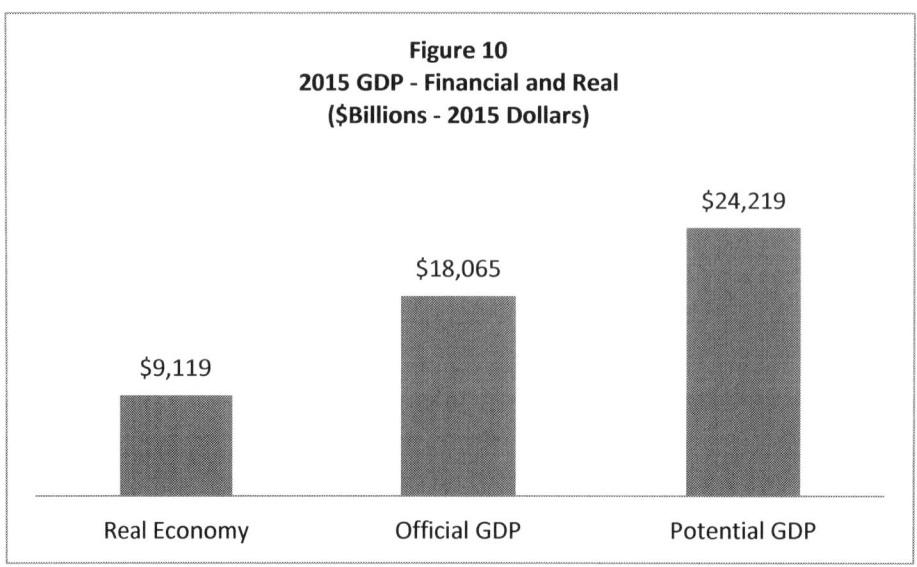

Source: Author's calculation based on excess profits, and lost production value from slow growth.

($Billions - 2015 Dollars)		
Real Economy	$9,119	
		$1,000 Oil Speculation
		$7,946 Excess Financial Growth
Excess Profits	$8,946	
Official GDP	$18,065	
Slow Growth - Lost Value	$6,154	
Potential GDP	$24,219	

Source: Author's calculation based on figures 8 and 9, and estimate of cost of oil speculation between 2004 and 2013.

Real Economy as Percent of Official GDP: 50%

Real Economy as Percent of Potential GDP: 38%

Figure 10 shows a value estimate of the real economy, compared to official GDP.

Excess financial growth accounts for $7.9 trillion of GDP growth reported since 1973.

Without hard data on the cost of oil speculation, I used a conservative figure of $1 trillion dollars for the period between 2004 and 2013.

These figures combined total more than $8.9 trillion in excess profits.

Officially reported GDP, minus the value of excess profits equals the value of the real economy.

Note that the real economy estimate is only 50 percent of the GDP value reported in official statistics.

This assessment shows how the real economy only makes up half of the New Economy.

The composition of growth has changed, such that excess financial growth has transformed the economy.

Combined Impact
If the economy had grown at the historic average rate established in the hundred years after the civil war, the value of GDP in 2015 would have been higher by $6.1 trillion dollars.

Adding that $6.1 trillion to the officially reported GDP generates potential GDP, which is the GDP the economy would have reached, if the historic average rate of growth had been maintained.

The difference between potential GDP and the real economy is more than $15 trillion dollars.

Slow and distorted growth has transformed society, and left us with a $15 trillion dollar hole in the economy.

The economy today is growing at less than 60 percent of the historic average rate of growth that prevailed from the 1870s to the 1970s.

Without large scale investment, there is no chance the historic 3.4 percent rate of growth, which defined America as an industrial power, can be restored.

Yet, there isn't enough demand in the economy to justify private sector investment.

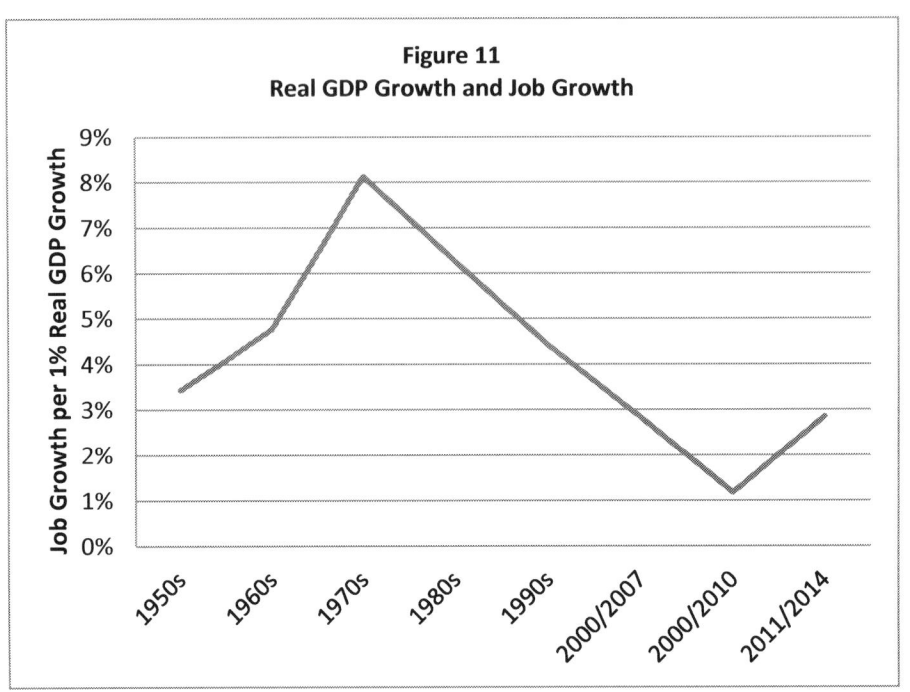

Source: Based on Laura D'Andrea Tyson, "Jobs Deficit, Investment Deficit, Fiscal Deficit," New York Times, Economix, July 29, 2011. The percentage increase in employment reflects the net employment change as a share of total employment in the base year (e.g., 1980 for the 1980s). Updated figures for 2000s and 2011 - 2014 based on data from Bureau of Economic Analysis and Bureau of Labor Statistics.

Decoupling of GDP Growth and Employment
Yet another trend that reflects uncanny consistency over time has been the progressive decoupling of GDP growth and the growth of employment.

For example, in the 1960s every percentage point growth in real GDP was matched by a corresponding 4.8 percent growth in employment.

This jobs/GDP ratio is a measure of the relationship between GDP growth and job growth.

In the 1970s the ratio increased to 8.1 percent.

While both wages and the jobs/GDP ratio peaked in the 1970s, since then both have shown progressive decline.

In the 1980s every percentage point of GDP growth was matched by a corresponding 6.25 percent growth in employment, a decline of nearly 25 percent compared to the 1970s.

In the 1990s employment grew by 4.4 percent for every percentage gain in GDP, only a little more than half the rate of the 1970s.

From 2000 to 2007 the ratio fell to 2.8 percent, which was a little more than a third of the jobs/GDP ratio in the 1970s.

For the period 2000-2010 the ratio was just 1.2 percent, or roughly 15 percent of the jobs/GDP ratio shown for the 1970s.

Figure 11 reflects a long term trend in which GDP growth has become decoupled from growth in employment.

For nearly 40 years, the economy's capacity to create jobs progressively declined.

From 2011 through 2014, the jobs/GDP ratio re-bounded, to a little more than 2.8 percent.

That recovery puts the ratio back on par with where it was in the period between 2000 and 2007, but still only a little more than a third of the jobs/GDP ratio in the 1970s.

Compared to the 1970s, the economy's capacity to create jobs has declined by 65 percent.

That's what I call stagnation.

Since 1994, the rate of economic growth has been 26 percent slower than the historic average.

Paul Craig Roberts has made an astute observation about recessions and the potential impact of government policy tools like tax cuts and lower interest rates.

Businesses historically tend to lay off workers in bad times and increase hiring in good times.

But thanks to offshoring, companies that previously had operations in this country have been relocated overseas.

No matter what government might do, companies can't increase hiring when they no longer have operations here that could potentially create jobs.

The study of business cycles is centrally concerned with how businesses respond to the economic environment and to government policy.

Because government policy has no impact on business operations that are no longer here, government policies that might otherwise support economic recovery are no longer effective.

Could it be that offshoring isn't really good for the American economy after all?

Food for Thought

Between 1980 and 1986, the price of oil fell by 71 percent, while the rate of inflation fell by 70 percent.

Yet, it was monetary policy that was given credit for overcoming inflation.

In 1979 Federal Reserve chair Paul Volcker imposed very high interest rates to induce recession—to create high unemployment as a way of stopping the growth of wages.

In 1987 the appointment of Alan Greenspan as Fed chairman served to institutionalize this anti-inflation policy of creating artificially high unemployment to prevent inflation.

The rate of growth Greenspan considered non-inflationary was slower by more than $1/4^{th}$ compared to the historic average that established this country as an industrial power.

Anti-inflation policy is equivalent to slow growth policy.

Slow and distorted growth has cost the U.S. economy more than $15 trillion dollars in lost production.

Compared to the 1970s, the economy today is marked by
- 65% decline in jobs created for every percentage point of GDP, and
- $1.3 trillion dollar decline in *annual* wages, paid as a proportion of GDP

Meanwhile, corporate profits have more than doubled since the 1980s, while the rate of business investment is less than half the rate of the 1960s.

Excess profits and too little demand are two sides of the same coin.

The economy suffers from stagnant wages and too little demand, because corporations have used profits to make *financial* investments instead of *job creating* investments in manufacturing.

Logic of the New Economy

Main Points

The U.S. economy has been transformed by a process of *financialization*, in which financial expansion has become the primary source of growth.

The origins of the process were
- anti-inflation policy, and
- expansion of the credit market

Anti-inflation policy brought a realignment of interests between the Federal Reserve and the financial sector.

Long after the threat of high inflation had passed, Fed policy continued to protect financial interests at the expense of productive industry.

The Federal Reserve approved reductions in reserve requirements that expanded the credit market to more than $50 trillion dollars.

While slow and distorted growth have cost the real economy $15 trillion of lost value, expansion of credit has established debt financed consumption as the engine of growth.

Total outstanding credit market debt doubled between 1999 and 2007, while corporate profits also doubled in the same period.

Financial profits as a share of corporate profits today are more than twice the level of the 1980s.

Financial profits accounted for only 15 percent of GDP in 1950, compared to 45 percent for manufacturing.

By 2007, financial profits accounted for 44 percent of GDP, compared to 15 percent for manufacturing.

The importance of the 1970s and the Carter / Reagan embrace of deregulation is that the origins of the change were thoroughly bipartisan.

Republicans glorify the legacy of deregulation, while Democrats rarely mention deregulation in the Carter administration.

The result is that neither party mentions the comprehensive deregulation bills Carter signed into law before Reagan took office.

Anti-inflation Policy
Both Carter and Reagan agreed with Volcker's use of tight money policy to deliberately induce recession, and use high unemployment to overcome inflation.

This bipartisanship marked a fundamental transformation in which the goal of government policy changed, from pursing high growth and full employment, to maintaining low inflation.

This shift in priorities, from high growth and full employment, to one of *anti-inflation* policy, created a fundamental deficit in the growth of demand.

The old model is shown in the virtuous circle of growth.

As the growth of productivity drives rising wages, higher incomes create more demand-led growth and more employment.

Larger markets create incentive for more investment that raises productivity, thereby supporting higher wages and driving the upward spiral of growth.

The New Economy model is outlined in the circle of stagnation.

When wages stopped growing in the 1970s, the logic of the demand generating process was altered.

With stagnant demand the incentive for *productive* investment declined, while excess profit was allocated instead to financial investments that were essentially speculative.

Manufacturing and small business are most profitable in an environment of moderate unemployment and mild inflation.

The reason is that high unemployment brings a fall in consumption, which serves to undermine profits and acts as disincentive for productive investment.

In contrast, high unemployment and low inflation serve the interests of the financial sector.

Inflation erodes the value of money used to pay back loans, and thereby erodes the value of financial assets.

For example, consider a mortgage with an interest rate of eight percent.

Annual inflation of five percent would result in a yield of only three percent on the mortgage.

This is because the rate on the mortgage is only three percent higher than the rate of inflation:

(8% mortgage – 5% inflation = 3% yield).

If inflation falls to two percent, the effective yield on the mortgage doubles, because the rate on the mortgage would be six percent higher than the rate of inflation:

(8% mortgage - 2% inflation = 6% yield).

A mortgage is a financial asset, which rises in value as inflation falls.

Beginning in the late 1970s, Volcker's priority of overcoming inflation created a realignment of interests, because *anti-inflation* policy serves the finance sector, at the expense of productive industry.

Because the name of the bank includes the word "Federal," there is a common misconception that the Fed is a government agency.

In fact, the Federal Reserve is a system of 12 regional banks, which are owned by private commercial banks.

The 12 regional banks (Boston, New York, Philadelphia, Richmond, Atlanta, Dallas, Denver, St. Louis, Kansas City, Chicago, Minnesota, and San Francisco), are locally owned and controlled.

Prior to the 1970s, members of the Fed Board of Governors were influenced by Keynesian economics, and supported the use of government stimulus to maintain demand.

Volcker imposed high interest rates to induce recession, which amounted to using high unemployment to overcome inflation.

This brought a re-alignment of interests, in which official policy became far more compatible with the interests of the financial sector.

Even so, Volcker was uncomfortable with wholesale deregulation of finance, and cautioned against the dangers of speculation.

Banks were making high risk loans to fund corporate take overs and leveraged buyouts.

Volcker wanted to put limits on the use of borrowed money to buy the stock of companies targeted for hostile takeover.

The mechanism was to impose margin rules like those applied to stock trading, which would limit the use of borrowed money to buy equity in target companies.

The Fed chairman was outvoted by Reagan appointees to the Board of Governors, who opposed the restrictions.

Volcker also opposed the repeal of Glass-Steagall restrictions on commercial banks, which benefited from federal insured deposits, as well as access to capital at low interest provided by the Federal Reserve.

Glass-Steagall prohibited commercial banks from engaging in investment banking, which had contributed to the speculative boom that led to the 1929 crash.

In 1987 Volcker was again outvoted, when the Fed approved an exemption allowing commercial banks to sell securities.

Volcker then resigned, followed by Reagan's appointment of Alan Greenspan as the new Fed chairman.

The new chairman has been described as wanting to match Volcker's reputation as someone willing to use high unemployment to keep inflation low.

Greenspan raised interest rates in September 1987, but within a month was faced with the October crash of the stock market.

The Fed responded by buying short term Treasury notes, as a way of providing liquidity to banks.

Foreign central banks followed step, and within a few months the greater liquidity had stabilized the markets.

Thereafter, the rate on federal funds loaned to banks rose from 6.5 percent in early 1988 to more than 9 percent by the end of the year.

After mid-year 1989 Greenspan began cutting rates, but expressed concern over the prevailing *4 percent rate of inflation.*

Greenspan's appointment as Fed chairman served to institutionalize the priority of minimizing inflation.

Despite clear signs of recession, rates were lowered only marginally, from 8 percent in early 1990 to 7 percent by the end of the year.

By September 1992 the rate had been cut to 3 percent, but with only minimal impact on the economy.

In November 1992 the unemployment rate stood at 7.7 percent, arguably costing George H.W. Bush his bid for re-election.

After the first year of the Clinton administration, unemployment began falling as the economy entered the early stages of recovery.

Greenspan's response was to raise the federal funds rate six times in the course of a year, from 3 percent in January 1994 to 5.9 percent in February 1995.

Greenspan's justification for this near doubling of short term interest rates was that the economy was approaching the natural rate of unemployment, which would be inflationary.

The idea of a natural rate of unemployment originated in the late 1960s and was referenced in the 1970 Economic Report of the President.

In that year the report defined the benchmark for full employment as 3.8 percent.

In 1979 the official definition of full employment was 5.1 percent, and in 1983 was revised to the "inflation threshold unemployment rate" defined as a range between 6 and 7 percent.

Over time the so called natural rate nearly doubled, while Greenspan used interest rates to keep unemployment well above the rate of inflation.

The reason was to prevent unemployment from falling to a level that might bring wage growth, and potentially spark inflation.

Prior to the late 1990's, Federal Reserve policy promoted the financial sector over productive industry, while essentially endorsing stagnant wages and rising unemployment.

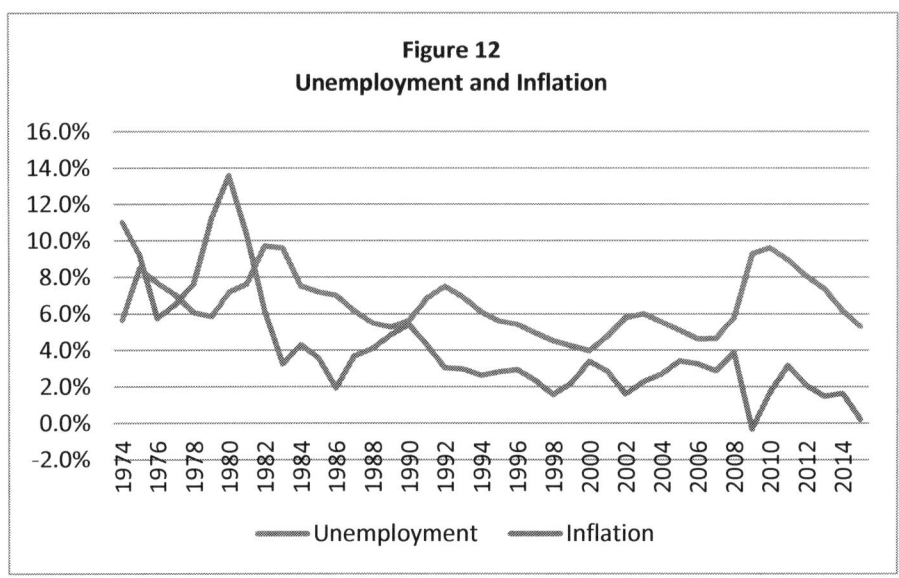

Source: Bureau of Labor Statistics.

Figure 12 shows official rates of unemployment and inflation.

The lines crossed in 1982, when the unemployment rate rose above the rate of inflation.

Since then the rate of unemployment has been maintained at levels higher than the rate of inflation.

In his 1997 address before Congress, Alan Greenspan described his priority of anticipating trends that could be inflationary, and taking pro-active measures to offset them.

The priority of anti-inflation policy was also reflected in official government projections that described *2.5 percent growth in GDP as the non-inflationary target for growth*.

Annual GDP growth of 2.5 percent is *26 percent slower* than the historic average rate of growth that prevailed when America became an industrial power.

For more than 15 years, the Federal Reserve used interest rates to maintain low inflation, which was accompanied by slow growth and the loss of productive output.

Slow growth and high unemployment, designed as *anti-inflation* policy, was the hallmark of the New Economy before the boom in stock prices that developed in the mid 1990s.

As we've seen, the Volcker legacy of *anti-inflation* policy was maintained by Alan Greenspan in the decade that followed.

But Greenspan's views on financial regulation were vastly different than his predecessor, and those views ultimately created a perfect storm that unfolded in the 2008 financial crisis.

Debt Driven Growth
Thomas Palley describes the role of finance in the New Economy as an unintended consequence of what he calls the demand gap.

The demand gap is the difference between consumption based on income, and consumption based on credit and long term debt.

Deregulation brought financial innovation that created new debt instruments and provided more leverage.

The effect was to offset the gap in demand, by creating more debt.

As real incomes stopped growing, households aided by the new role of women in the workplace relied on ever greater leverage to acquire unprecedented levels of debt.

As a percentage of GDP, household debt was more than 26 times higher in 2010 than it was in 1970.

As the real economy declined, the New Economy evolved to create a new dependency on debt expansion and inflation of asset prices for growth.

Richard Duncan describes the unprecedented growth of credit as the cause of fundamental change in the structure of the economy.

Three developments made this expansion of credit possible.

First, beginning in 1988 (under Alan Greenspan), liquidity ratios that required banks to set aside reserves in relation to outstanding loans were replaced by capital requirements.

Unlike liquidity ratios, these capital requirements weren't based on liquid assets.

Instead, requirements were based on what was essentially an accounting entry showing the difference between the book value of assets and liabilities.

The result was a dramatic reduction in liquidity.

Liquidity ratios measure how sound banks are in their ability to pay short term obligations out of cash.

In 1945, commercial banks had reserves and vault cash equivalent to 12 percent of assets, with most assets held in low risk government bonds.

This meant the banking sector as a whole had a liquidity ratio of 12 percent.

In 2007, this liquidity ratio of bank reserves to total assets was only 0.6 percent, at a time when bank assets were held in high risk derivatives and mortgage backed securities.

This enormous increase in leverage was a principle cause of the financial crisis that unfolded in 2008.

Second, new forms of credit that evolved in the 1980s were also subject to requirements based not on liquidity but on capital, applied to commercial banks and other financial firms as well.

For example, asset backed securities refer to loans (mortgage loans, student loans, credit card loans) that are bundled as securities and sold to investors.

In 2007, mortgage backed securities with AA ratings were subject to a capital requirement of only 1.6 percent.

This meant a seller of AA mortgage backed securities was required to have capital backing (on paper) of only $1,600 for every $100,000 of securities sold.

At the end of 2007, Fannie Mae and Freddie Mac had nearly $5 trillion of mortgage assets, either held on their books or backed through loan guarantees made to third party lenders.

The requirement for Fannie Mae was capital equivalent to 1.5 percent of assets, with the value of assets based on the book value of mortgages in Fannie's portfolio.

Likewise, the requirement for Freddie Mac was capital equivalent to only 1.3 percent of assets.

Adopting capital requirements in place of liquidity ratios established a system Richard Duncan calls issuing credit without reserves.

By removing the requirement to set aside liquid cash in reserve, this change allowed the financial system to create an unprecedented volume of credit – over $50 trillion of debt in 2007.

At the same time, this extraordinary expansion of credit was issued by highly leveraged financial institutions, and then sold in the form of debt instruments to highly leveraged investors.

Selling the debt generated cash, which was then used to issue new credit, buy up more debt, and repeat the process in a continuous cycle of credit creation.

Overall, easy credit at low interest created a path to generating wealth through taking out loans and using the borrowed money to buy assets.

This path to making money was used not only by individuals, but by corporations as well.

Total credit market debt doubled between 1999 and 2007, while corporate profits also doubled in the same period.

A third development driving credit expansion was an unprecedented increase in foreign currency, which was issued by foreign central banks and used to buy U.S. dollar assets.

Between 1997 and 2007, foreign central banks provided nearly $4 trillion dollars in credit to the U.S. market.

Of that $4 trillion total, some $1.3 trillion was invested in U.S. Treasury bonds, while another $929 billion was invested in mortgage backed securities sold by Fannie Mae and Freddie Mac.

The remainder of nearly $2 trillion dollars was invested in corporate bonds and the U.S. stock market.

These investments impacted the U.S. economy by driving up prices in stock values and house prices.

For example, the Dow Jones Industrial Average rose from 6,000 in 1996, to 14,000 in 2007.

While average stock prices more than doubled, the median price of a single family home rose 77 percent, from $140,000 in 1996 to $248,000 in 2007.

Excess liquidity also served to put downward pressure on interest rates.

The Federal Reserve raised the fed funds rate (rate charged on loans made to banks) 17 times between June 2004 and June 2006.

These rate hikes were intended to raise mortgage rates and slow down the housing boom.

But there was so much money flowing into the system, that there was no impact on the housing market.

Expanding the Service Economy
Unprecedented expansion of credit brought a shift in the focus of economic activity, from producing goods to providing services.

For example, manufacturing value added declined from 26 percent of GDP in 1948 to only 12 percent in 2007.

In the same period, the service sector more than doubled in relation to the size of the economy overall.

Consider three segments of the service sector:
- Finance, insurance, and real estate,
- Information, professional and business services, and
- Education and health services

These three categories combined accounted for 19 percent of GDP in 1948, but made up 46 percent of GDP in 2007.

This change in the contribution to GDP has been matched by a corresponding change in the distribution of employment.

In 2007 more than two thirds of all jobs were in service sector occupations, while employment in manufacturing was actually lower than in 1948.

The historic expansion of credit, which occurred in a period of prolonged stagnation in wages, financed the rise in services and the purchase of manufactured imports from low wage countries

Unintended Consequences
The 1970s stagnation created a focus on reducing labor costs to reduce inflation.

Financial deregulation progressed in tandem with deregulation of industry, while unregulated new forms of finance emerged.

With expanded credit and financial deregulation, the result was that companies made profits from offshoring, downsizing, mergers and acquisitions, and other forms of financial engineering.

These changes marked the beginning of a new era of financialization, in which expanded production has been replaced by expansion of finance as the primary source of growth.

Financialization has brought fundamental restructuring of the economy, by undermining wages and slowing down the overall rate of growth.

In the process, the agency role of government has been transformed, because the interests represented by official policy have changed.

With *anti-inflation* policy at the Federal Reserve, official policy has abandoned the goal of industrial expansion and full employment.

Instead, official policy of both Republican and Democratic administrations, promotes credit expansion and debt financed consumption as the engine of growth.

This New Economy model of growth serves the interests of the finance sector, at the expense of productive industry.

The next section will show the impact of the process, followed by the logic of policy to maintain it.

Food for Thought

Anti-inflation policy serves financial sector interests, at the expense of productive industry.

Moderate unemployment and mild inflation create an environment that is most profitable for manufacturing and small business.

In contrast, high unemployment brings a fall in consumption, which undermines profits and acts as disincentive for productive investment.

Anti-inflation policy uses high unemployment to keep inflation at very low levels.

Low inflation protects the value of financial assets, such as mortgages, and thereby serves Wall Street financial interests.

Between the early 1980s and the mid-1990s, *anti-inflation* policy created an explicit alliance between the Federal Reserve and Wall Street.

While the Federal Reserve is owned by commercial banks, Fed policy in the post war period was far more closely aligned with productive industry.

In the same period of *anti-inflation* policy, financial deregulation established a system of creating credit without reserves.

The unprecedented expansion of credit and the lack of regulation spurred a new kind of growth, driven more by financial engineering than by expansion of production.

At the same time, non-financial firms became increasingly oriented toward financial profits, spending nearly three times more on stock trading than on productive investment.

Production has now been shifted to low wage countries, while slow growth in the U.S. economy is driven by financialization.

Wall Street Rules

Main Points

Four developments aided the process of financialization:
- Deregulation of industry,
- Financial deregulation,
- Non-regulation of new financial products, and
- New accounting rules applied to both financial firms and non-financial corporations

These developments created a mutually reinforcing process, in which financial interests gained control of productive industry.

Shareholder value promoted the goal of maximizing liquidity, as a means of maximizing stock prices on behalf of shareholders.

Executive compensation was shifted to stock options, to align the interests of management with the interests of shareholders.

Financial derivatives emerged as a tool used to report current earnings based on *projections* of future income.

Repeal of Glass-Steagall created incentives for banks to make off balance sheet loans to companies in which they held stock.

Deregulation of telecommunications and massive overinvestment spawned a boom in the stock of telecom and internet companies.

New accounting rules allowed firms to use pension plans to fund operating expenses.

The process created incentives for corporate restructuring through downsizing, offshoring, mergers and acquisitions, and financial engineering.

The end result was a new dominance of financial interests over productive industry.

In the context of *anti-inflation* policy and expanded credit, these developments elevated the role of finance and established debt fueled consumption as the basis for growth.

The logic of the New Economy was spawned by a fundamental change in the agency role of government.

Consistent with the lessons of the Great Depression, Keynesian economics is centrally concerned with government intervention as a response to market failure.

In the decades that followed the Depression, providing for the general welfare was understood as promoting full employment.

But in the 1970s, the combined onset of inflation and unemployment was interpreted as a case of government failure, in that regulation came to be seen as interfering with the natural balance of market forces.

Thereafter, deregulation of industry made it possible to cut wages and reduce the cost of employees seen as a prime source of inflation.

When Alan Greenspan replaced Paul Volcker at the Federal Reserve, expansion of credit was used to offset artificially high rates of unemployment, which had been crafted as a tool of anti-inflation policy.

At the same time, Greenspan promoted the idea of efficient and self-regulating markets, and opposed government regulation in every form.

The result was a transformation in the agency role of government, in which policy shifted away from representing productive industry and its associated workforce, to representing financial interests.

This changed orientation in government policy, was matched by changes in the private sector, which transformed the agency role of corporations and elevated the financial sector as the prime driver of the New Economy.

Financialization is a process in which the finance sector becomes increasingly important in the economy.

The process has been fostered through two interlocking and self-reinforcing channels.

The first channel has been through economic policy.

The Federal Reserve's *anti-inflation policy* promoted finance sector interests over those of productive industry.

As we've seen, interest rates were used to maintain unemployment at artificially high levels, with the explicit goal of keeping inflation below 4 percent.

Second, the Federal Reserve's use of capital requirements (on paper) in place of liquidity ratios gave banks more leverage and established a system of creating credit without reserves.

The result was expansion of credit to more than $50 trillion dollars, such that demand was driven by consumption based on debt.

The third channel was through financial deregulation, as well as non-regulation of newly developed financial products.

The combined result was a public policy environment that facilitated the increased dominance of finance over productive industry.

This chapter will examine inter-related processes that drove the transformation in both financial and non-financial business.

In the early 1980s, deregulation of savings and loans created a market for junk bonds issued to finance leveraged buy outs (LBOs).

LBOs were hostile takeovers financed with borrowed money, which targeted firms with high operating costs.

The takeover movement forced firms to adopt defensive strategies that included streamlining operations through downsizing, and taking on debt to increase cash reserves.

This defensive strategy became synonymous with the culture of *shareholder value*, in which the role of management is to maximize the firm's *present value*.

By definition, a company's present value is a function of its future value.

Investing in long term growth will increase a company's future value, at the expense of its present value.

Withholding those investments will increase present value, at the expense of future value.

Shareholder value embodies the goal of *maximizing present value* by *maximizing liquidity*.

The process generates higher prices for company shares, creating maximum *short term* gain for shareholders.

Executive compensation in the form of stock options created incentives designed to align the interests of management with the goal of maximizing share value.

Financial derivatives were used in ways that allowed companies to report *current earnings* based on *projections of future income*.

Repeal of Glass-Steagall allowed the expanded credit available to banks to be allocated, not to more lending, but instead to speculation in highly leveraged financial investments.

This policy environment of expanded credit and financial deregulation also contributed to speculative bubbles that emerged in the internet and telecommunications sectors.

Finally, pursuit of high stock prices was aided by new accounting rules that allowed shifting of assets from defined benefit pension plans to defined contribution 401(k) plans.

In sum, new financial products were created to increase leverage and widen the range of assets that could be used as collateral.

For example, while employees can't borrow against pension plans, they can and do take out loans against the value of 401(k) retirement plans.

With access to expanded credit and a broader range of assets in savings plans, increased leverage fueled the rise of the finance sector, and led to Wall Street's dominance over productive industry.

Through understanding these interrelated processes of *financialization*, we can better assess both their impact and relevance in the context of macroeconomic policy carried out by the Federal Reserve.

Financial Deregulation
The inflation of the 1970s, along with high interest rates imposed to combat it, led to a series of changes that brought substantial deregulation of finance.

In the context of high inflation, regulations that limited bank interest rates essentially forced depositors to lose money on savings accounts that paid low fixed rates.

In 1972 the SEC granted an exemption that allowed Merrill Lynch, a securities firm, to offer shares to investors in money market mutual funds.

These funds operated much like bank accounts, but offered higher returns than the interest rates banks were allowed to pay.

State chartered banks also began paying interest on checking accounts, which state regulators were inclined to allow for banks in their jurisdictions.

Over time, as depositors looked for higher interest alternatives to bank deposits, Congress repealed the restrictions on interest rates banks could charge.

Credit markets were also evolving in tandem with the new system of floating exchange rates that determined currency values.

Floating exchange rates created the foreign exchange market, which provided a new vehicle for speculation and potentially high returns.

Foreign banks had also begun accumulating large reserves of dollars well before Nixon revoked the gold standard, while reserves increased greatly thereafter under floating exchange rates.

Dollars outside the country were concentrated in the Eurodollar market in London and were used to recycle profits from oil revenues into loans made to developing countries.

These petrodollar loans carried higher risk but were far more profitable than traditional bank lending.

In the same period, large corporations began bypassing banks by taking out commercial loans in the financial markets.

This commercial paper market increased in volume from $4.5 billion in 1960 to $90 billion in 1979, and then more than doubled to over $200 billion in 1985.

Banks also faced increasing competition from nonbank entities.

Examples include credit card companies, as well as finance divisions of large retailers like Sears and J.C. Penny, and auto makers that began financing vehicle sales.

Inflation reduced profits from lending for banks, and even more so for savings and loan associations (S&Ls) that held assets in fixed rate mortgages.

In 1980, financial deregulation was initiated under Carter with the passage of the Depository Institutions Deregulation and Monetary Control Act.

The act removed Regulation Q restrictions on interest rates banks could pay on customer deposits, as well as restrictions on interest rates charged on loans.

S&Ls were granted the right to make commercial loans, provide the same NOW accounts offered by brokerages and other lenders, and to issue credit cards.

Deregulation continued under Reagan, with the 1981 passage of the Economic Recovery Tax Act.

Thereafter, S&Ls were allowed to sell their mortgages and invest the proceeds in higher yield government bonds.

The 1982 Garn-St. Germain Depository Institutions Act further deregulated the S&Ls by raising the proportion of assets that could be held in commercial and consumer loans.

The act also lifted restrictions on the types of securities S&Ls were allowed to buy.

Within a short period, S&Ls became heavily invested in junk bonds, which had been created by Wall Street financier Michael Milken.

In the 1980s, junk bonds were used to finance leveraged buyouts (LBOs), in which borrowed money was used to buy companies.

Takeover artists borrowed money to buy stock in a target company (using the stock as collateral), and would then sell off assets and company cash flow to pay down the debt.

Using junk bonds, raiders could put up $6 million (3%) to buy a $200 million dollar company.

By the mid-1980s, S&Ls had diversified into a wide range of questionable investments, including large loans in commercial real estate and holdings of some $150 billion in junk bonds.

A critical element of the Garn-St. Germain Act was a provision that extended the amortization period applied to asset sales, from 10 years to 40 years.

The intent was to facilitate mergers, by making it easier to buy troubled S&Ls that held assets based on low interest, fixed-rate real estate loans.

In practice, the change encouraged real estate lending that wasn't profitable, while creating the appearance of solvency for S&Ls that had more liabilities than assets.

Between 1986 and 1989, nearly 300 S&Ls were closed by the Federal Savings and Loan Insurance Corporation (FSLIC).

In 1989, Congress passed the Financial Institutions Reform, Recovery, and Enforcement Act (FIRREA).

The act created the Resolution Trust Corporation as a federal trust designated to pay off creditors and depositors for bankrupt S&Ls.

Between 1989 and 1995, nearly 750 S&Ls were closed by the Resolution Trust Corporation.

With the 1989 passage of FIRREA, federal regulators changed the rules so that S&Ls could no longer buy junk bonds.

This brought collapse of the junk bond market, and bankruptcy for Milken's investment firm, Drexel Burnham Lambert, in 1992.

The takeover movement of the 1980s marked a critical juncture, in which deregulation (and non-regulation) of finance created the impetus for profound changes in non-financial businesses.

In 1989, Michael Jensen of the Harvard Business School published a paper on the "Eclipse of the Public Corporation."

Jensen argued that the LBO craze was the expression of an efficient market.

The idea was that selling off corporate divisions and subsidiaries would maximize profits.

The combined value of stock *for divisions sold separately* was greater than the value of a single stock that reflected those same divisions operating as a combined company.

As an example, in 1986 the investment firm Kravis, Kohlberg, Roberts (KKR) bought the Safeway grocery chain for $4.3 billion.

Using only $2 million of its own money, KKR made $65 million in fees, and received 20 percent of profits from any subsequent sale.

Safeway was then downsized by selling off entire divisions and eliminating 63,000 employees.

Jensen's argument was that Safeway's true value (defined as *shareholder* value) had been "unlocked."

In fact, the emergence of the takeover movement signaled a transfer of power, in which the financial sector was allowed to use the leverage of junk bonds to gain control over productive industry.

In the year prior to the takeover, Safeway had posted record profits of $235 million dollars.

There was no credible case to be made that Safeway was inefficient, or to support the KKR assertion that the company had failed to keep up with "global competition."

Quite the contrary, using junk bonds to finance takeovers emerged as a new technique of gaining corporate control.

In reality it was not a company's profitability, but instead simply its liquidity that determined whether it could become a potential takeover target.

At the same time, the extraordinary leverage of the LBO meant the size of the potential takeover was no longer an issue.

In 1989, KKR orchestrated the takeover of RJR Nabisco for $31.4 billion, which was the largest in history at the time, marking the dawn of a new era in which the size of the target company no longer mattered.

Karen Ho is an anthropologist and former analyst for Banker's Trust. In *Liquidated: An Ethnography of Wall Street*, she describes the impact of the takeover movement:

> "LBOs generated such an environment of fear that corporations restructured themselves in anticipation of takeover attempts, hoping to raise their stock prices and render themselves less vulnerable to the restructuring rationales of corporate raiders."

It was this changed environment, fueled by unregulated innovation in finance, and by Greenspan's expansion of credit, that transformed American business.

Shareholder Value
In the 1980s, the upswing in LBOs, re-branded as mergers and acquisitions, took place on such scale to be described as "merger mania."

Between 1979 and 1989 there were more than 17,000 mergers and acquisitions, with a reported transaction value of $1.3 trillion dollars.

The LBO craze led to an increasing corporate emphasis on promoting the interests of shareholders, or those who own shares of corporate stock.

Business culture had for decades endorsed the view of corporate responsibility as centrally concerned with the interests of stakeholders.

Stakeholders are defined as customers, employees, suppliers, and communities that are all seen as having a stake in corporate success.

In the 1980s, corporate boards and CEOs began focusing almost exclusively on *short term stock performance* as the primary goal of the business organization.

A turning point for corporate culture was a 1981 speech by General Electric (GE) CEO Jack Welch, on the subject of "Growing Fast in a Slow-Growth Economy."

Welch was insistent that aggressive cost cutting would be required to raise profits, and that profit margins should drive decisions on whether to sell off underperforming lines of business.

Welch transformed GE, from a real economy company with a large workforce, to a downsized company with a substantial base in financial services.

In 1980, GE reported $25 billion in revenue with net earnings of $1.5 billion, which was 6 percent of revenue.

In 1998, the company reported $100 billion in revenue with net earnings of $9.3 billion, or 9.3 percent of revenue.

For the period as a whole, net revenues increased by $7.8 billion dollars.

The change was accompanied by rising prices for GE stock, as well as praise for the new found religion of shareholder value.

First, the company was restructured through a process of sales and acquisitions.

GE was founded on the goal of commercializing the inventions of Thomas Edison, which served to develop markets for electrical products.

By the 1920s, GE had become one of the largest companies in the world, producing turbines, generators, transformers, electric motors, light bulbs, and small electrical appliances.

When Welch was appointed CEO in the early 1980s, company profits were based on traditional lines of business.

These included airplane engines, kitchen appliances, industrial products, power generation equipment, and high-tech products such as medical devices.

Welch sold off hundreds of productive lines of business that included small appliances, central air conditioning, consumer electronics, aerospace, and mining operations.

In the same period, there were dozens of acquisitions of financial services companies, as well as insurance companies and leasing businesses.

By 1998, over 40 percent of company profits were based on the operations of GE Financial Services.

This process of restructuring also reduced the workforce by nearly a third, cutting 120,000 employees from the 1980 level of 411,000.

As a result, revenue per employee rose from $62,000 in 1981 to just under $343,000 in 1998, a more than five-fold increase in less than 20 years.

The smaller workforce, achieved largely by selling off manufacturing lines of business, is estimated to have saved between $5 billion and $7 billion in operating costs.

Thus, much of the $7.8 billion expansion in earnings was created through downsizing and the sale of large workforce lines of business.

Second, Welch's tenure was marked by substantial cuts in research and development.

As a percent of revenue, GE expenditure on R&D went from over 3 percent in the early 1980s, to 1.5 percent in 1998.

If the level of R&D expenditure had been maintained, GE would have spent an additional $1.5 billion on R&D in 1998.

Instead, $1.5 billion that wasn't spent on R&D contributed to the $7.8 billion expansion in reported earnings.

Third, Welch's largest investment was in allocating $30 billion dollars to fund buy backs of GE stock.

Stock buy backs raise the price of shares, and thereby contribute to the immediate enhancement of quarterly earnings statements.

But this short term goal of higher prices for company stock is fundamentally at odds with the goal of long term growth.

The use of $30 billion to buy back company shares meant $30 billion was not used to expand the company's output, either through
- investments in plant and equipment, or
- creating new products to increase market share, which is the purpose of R&D.

In 2000, Allan Kennedy published *The End of Shareholder Value*, which criticized the way GE had been restructured and argued Welch had mortgaged the company's future.

Kennedy also provided a detailed assessment indicating GE's stock was substantially over-valued.

During Welch's tenure, the price of GE stock (including a 3:1 stock split) rose by a factor of 42:1, from $1.20/share to more than $50/share.

The stock declined thereafter, reaching a record low of $8.51 per share in 2009.

In 2012, the average closing price was $20.16 per share, a decline of 60 percent from levels reached in 2000.

The long term assessment is that Welch created *the illusion* of a company that grew and became steadily more profitable over a period of 20 years.

Fundamentally, shareholder value has brought the pursuit of a high *share price* as a proxy for *share value*.

Long term growth creates wealth through expanded output and investments that raise profit through economies of scale.

Value added in production, investments that raise productivity, and returns from economies of scale have long been the hallmark of manufacturing.

But with high production costs and low profit margins, manufacturing became a casualty of the incentives for downsizing and offshoring created by the shareholder value revolution.

The tragedy of American industry is that Welch's strategy of downsizing was copied by hundreds of other companies.

In 1990, a Newsweek cover story reported on cost cutting and downsizing in the country's most profitable companies.

Ranked by the number of layoffs, these were:
General Motors – 74,000
IBM   –   60,000
Sears   –   50,000
AT&T   –   40,000
Boeing   –   28,000
Digital Equipment – 20,000

These companies weren't being downsized because they weren't profitable.

CEOs were laying off workers because downsizing made their companies *more valuable*, in terms of short term increase in stock prices.

In 2000, Kennedy estimated the top Fortune 500 companies following GE's downsizing accounted for some 20 percent of U.S. GDP.

The trend also provided the context for offshoring, as new investments in manufacturing were shifted to low wage countries.

Thus, the decline of American industry financed the rise in stock values, as corporate restructuring was used to support high prices for company shares.

American business has been captured by financial interests, because Wall Street writes the rules that become law.

In some cases, the rules are re-written through deregulation bills passed in Congress.

Other cases amount to non-regulation, in which nothing is done to regulate new modes of business that emerge in finance or the corporate sector.

Executive Compensation

The original sin that led to downsizing of production and financialization of business, was the linking of CEO pay to the value of stock options.

Over a ten year period at GE, Welch made over $400 million in salary, bonuses, and stock options.

In 2000 alone, at the height of the stock market boom, Welch made over $123 million.

In 2003, financial records obtained through divorce proceedings revealed Welch's retirement package was worth some $420 million dollars.

In 1978, the ratio of CEO pay to employee wages was 29:1, meaning the average CEO made as much as 29 employees made in a year.

In 2000, the ratio was 383:1, with the average CEO making as much as the combined income of nearly 400 employees.

In 2011, the average CEO made over $12 million, while many in the top 50 companies made between $30 million and $50 million a year.

Unprecedented compensation for CEOs has been funded with stock options, which are granted by corporate boards of directors.

In 1990, Michael Jensen argued that basing CEO compensation on stock options would serve to align the interests of management with those of shareholders.

The idea was that a company's true value was reflected in its *net present value*, expressed as earnings per share.

The way to maximize *net present value*, was to tie CEO pay to the value of company stock.

Driving stock prices higher would make the CEO rich, and maximize shareholder value at the same time.

CEOs were granted options worth millions of dollars if the stock rose, which was arguably consistent with the premise of aligning the interests of management with performance.

But in practice, CEOs were granted more options when stocks declined.

These options were granted at considerable cost to the companies involved.

In 1993, the Financial Accounting Standards Board (FASB) recommended a rule to require companies to deduct the cost of options from reported earnings.

What followed was a lobbying campaign to fight the rule, as well as bipartisan opposition to the FASB.

There was also opposition from the Clinton administration, led by Treasury Secretary Lloyd Bentsen and Commerce Secretary Ron Brown.

Faced with overwhelming bipartisan opposition, SEC chairman Arthur Levitt advised the FASB to back down.

In effect, CEOs were given incentives to cannibalize productive industry as a means of supporting higher prices for company stock.

In a subsequent repeat of 1993, the FASB passed a ruling in 2004 that would require companies to list stock options as an expense.

The House of Representatives voted to block the rule, which passed with overwhelming (312 to 111) support, and included Speaker of the House Nancy Pelosi (D-CA).

The upshot is that Wall Street lobbyists won the day, with bipartisan support in Congress.

Merrill Lynch estimated in 2001 that if leading technology companies were required to deduct the expense of options, reported profits would have been cut *by 60 percent*.

Wall Street rules designed to overstate earnings create over-valuation of company stock, which serves to inflate the value of stocks traded and the commissions earned on those trades.

American business has been captured by Wall Street, because CEOs have been paid to serve finance sector interests instead of making productive investments in domestic industry.

In 2004, the *International* Accounting Standards Board adopted a rule that required options to be deducted as expenses.

Later that year, the FASB was able to implement its corresponding rule 123R, which mandates expensing of options.

After a fight lasting more than a decade, it was action taken by the international community that prevented Congress from gutting the rule.

Derivatives and
Mark to Model Accounting
Derivatives are contracts that derive their value from the value of an underlying asset.

For example, a futures contract allows a farmer to lock in a safe price for his crop, based on assumptions in April as to what the price will be in August.

The farmer's contract protects him if the price falls, but also allows a speculator to gain if the price rises.

Futures contracts, based on commodities (wheat, corn, hog bellies, crude oil), have long been traded on regulated exchanges.

Common practice on a commodity exchange is to mark the value of a futures contract to current market value, on a daily basis.

This means using the current price of the underlying commodity to determine the value of the contract, each trading day, until the fulfillment date on the contract.

Futures contracts and *mark to market* rules on exchanges evolved as a way of trading contracts based on *commodities*, which are tangible items in the real economy.

In the early 1980s, banks began trading *financial* derivatives, which were based on underlying *financial* assets.

The most common were financial derivatives based on interest rates, and those based on exchange rates.

At the same time, new forms of financial derivatives were traded, not on exchanges, but through so called over-the-counter (OTC) transactions, which were not regulated.

Once the OTC market emerged, companies began using derivatives to either understate or overstate the true value of assets, depending on their needs in a given quarter.

Assets were valued through *mark to model* using estimates based on financial modeling. Ultimately, these models were manipulated through accounting fraud.

The figures recorded were based on *assumptions* about the future value of the underlying cash flow, meaning companies could report *current earnings* that were based on *projections*.

For CEOs compensated with stock options, the goal is to maximize the *net present value* of the firm.

With the use of financial derivatives and *mark to model* accounting, *current earnings* shown in company reports are valid, if and only if, *projections of future value* turn out to be true.

This insane practice was made possible by the non-regulation of derivatives, passed into law with the help of top Treasury Department officials and Federal Reserve chair Alan Greenspan.

In 1992, Congress passed the *Futures Trade Practices Act*.

The act granted the Commodity Futures Trading Commission (CFTC) the authority to exempt OTC derivatives from regulation.

In 1993, before leaving office, CFTC chair Wendy Gramm (wife of Texas senator Phil Gramm) exempted OTC derivatives from regulation.

Wendy Gramm was then awarded a seat on the board of directors of Enron, a company that was using derivatives to trade energy futures.

In 1994, the General Accounting Office (GAO) issued the results of a two year study calling for derivatives regulation, which included margin and reserve requirements on trades.

With Fed chairman Alan Greenspan and Clinton Treasury Secretary Lloyd Benson opposing the GAO recommendations, there was no action taken.

In 1995, President Clinton appointed the co-chair of Goldman Sachs, Robert Rubin, as Treasury Secretary.

Then in 1997, Clinton appointed Goldman's managing director, Gary Gensler, as Assistant Secretary for Financial Markets of the Treasury.

Against this backdrop of Treasury appointees from Goldman Sachs, in 1998 CFTC chair Brooksley Born proposed a study to evaluate the scale of potential risk posed by derivatives trading.

Later that year, Greenspan, Robert Rubin, and SEC chair Arthur Levitt won Congressional approval for a moratorium that temporarily suspended any CFTC action to regulate derivatives.

While Born ultimately resigned, Greenspan testified before Congress that unregulated markets in derivatives would create the perfect allocation of risk.

What seemed uncanny was the timing of two crises in derivatives trading, first at Barings Bank in the U.K., and then at Long Term Capital Management (LTCM), which was a Wall Street hedge fund.

In 1995, Barings (the oldest merchant bank in London at the time) collapsed when the bank's lead derivatives trader in Singapore lost some $1.3 billion trading futures contracts.

In 1998, LTCM suffered losses on exposure of well over $1 trillion in derivatives, at a time when the fund only had available capital of around $4 billion.

This unprecedented leverage was made possible by a legal loophole that provides regulatory exemption for hedge funds.

The Investment Company Act of 1940, established to regulate mutual funds, includes an exemption for private funds set up for wealthy investors.

The idea was that wealthy people were sophisticated investors who could do without the protections enforced through regulation.

The name "hedge fund" was coined in reference to a 1940s firm that followed a strategy of hedging the risk of short term investments with others that were held for the long term.

Easy credit and the booming stock market of the 1990s spawned a proliferation of hedge funds, which were not subject to disclosure requirements or to borrowing limits.

When LTCM collapsed, the fund had outstanding loans to dozens of Wall Street banks, while none of the banks knew the magnitude of leverage involved.

In September 1998, the chair of the New York Federal Reserve bank, working in concert with Alan Greenspan, brokered a deal in which the banks took over the fund and paid off the losses.

The LTCM case was historic, because the collapse of the fund posed a systemic threat to the financial system.

Yet it was less than a month later that Congress imposed a suspension that prevented any CFTC regulatory action on derivatives.

What followed was a two year lobbying campaign focused on passing legislation that would prevent regulation of derivatives.

In 2000, Senator Phil Gramm was one of 5 co-sponsors of the Commodity Futures Modernization Act (CFMA).

The final version of the bill included provisions later referred to as the "Enron loophole," which exempted derivatives based on energy futures from regulation.

Specific language in the bill was reportedly written by Enron lobbyists.

Ultimately, CFMA passed with strong bipartisan support in Congress, and was signed into law in December 2000 by President Clinton.

The law removed derivatives from the CFTC's regulatory authority, and exempted derivatives from regulation.

Regulatory exemption meant OTC derivatives were not subject to reporting requirements, or to congressional oversight.

At the time of the LTCM collapse in 1998, hedge fund assets were around $250 billion.

By 2006, the value of these unregulated funds had grown to an estimated $1.3 trillion.

That same year, hedge funds accounted for close to half the trading on the New York Stock Exchange (NYSE), and more than half the trading volume in derivatives.

The next step in the direct line from deregulation of derivatives to the 2008 financial crisis was to remove depression era restrictions on banks.

As was true in the case of derivatives and of de-regulation overall, the process was thoroughly bipartisan.

Repeal of Glass-Steagall
Robert Rubin began promoting the repeal of Glass-Steagall shortly after his appointment as Treasury Secretary in 1995.

With high inflation and increased competition in the 1970s, bank profits from lending had dramatically declined.

In the 1980s, the LBO craze was generating huge fees for investment banks that were not engaged in lending.

Investment banks were able to underwrite both the mergers involved and the subsequent breakup of merged companies when many were later found to be unprofitable.

Investment banks were also developing new investments in junk bonds as well as early forms of asset backed securities.

New financial products created a disadvantage for commercial banks, compared to firms engaged in investment banking, which were making enormous profits.

These changes led banks to pressure the Federal Reserve for exemptions to the Glass-Steagall separation between commercial and investment banking, which prohibited banks from dealing in securities.

The function of investment banking is to raise capital, which it does by underwriting and/or brokering new issues of corporate bonds and securities.

A bond is a debt instrument with a specified rate of return, as well as a future maturity date when the bond is to be paid.

Securities are most often shares of company stock, which give the buyer an equity position in the company selling the security.

The function of commercial banking is to provide credit, which it does by taking in deposits from households and businesses, and then using those federally insured deposits to make loans.

In 1984, the Secondary Mortgage Market Enhancement Act exempted investment firms from state regulations.

The law allowed investment banks to buy mortgages, and sell portions of the associated cash flows as securities.

The result was a profitable business for investment firms, but also the creation of a new "originate to distribute" lending model for banks and S&Ls.

A mortgage is a loan, which requires the lending institution to set aside reserves against the possibility of default.

When the bank can sell the mortgage to an investment firm, those reserves are freed up for additional lending.

The process creates profit incentive for banks to make loans, and then sell them to investment firms.

This meant the traditional gate-keeper function of banks, based on conservative assessment of the credit worthiness of borrowers, was transformed.

Because the loan would no longer be held by the bank, the traditional function of underwriters in evaluating risk was replaced.

Instead, securitization provided incentive for banks to perform the new function of making as many new loans as possible, regardless of risk, for the purpose of selling them.

In the late 1980s, the Federal Reserve began allowing commercial banks to underwrite corporate bonds, which had long been left to investment firms.

In 1994, Congress and the Clinton administration passed the Riegle-Neal Interstate Banking and Branching Efficiency Act.

The Act allowed branch bank operations nationwide, regardless of the home state in which a bank was incorporated.

What followed was a huge wave of bank mergers and acquisitions.

By the late 1990s, the Federal Reserve was allowing banks to acquire securities dealers.

The merger of Citicorp and Travelers Insurance was not legal at the time the deal was made in 1998.

But in 1999, with support from Greenspan, Rubin, and Larry Summers, Congress passed the Financial Services Modernization Act (FSMA).

Treasury Secretary Robert Rubin then resigned his position, and became vice chairman of the newly created Citigroup.

Rubin's move to Citigroup marked a stellar example of what has long been a revolving door, between Wall Street and top positions in government.

FSMA repealed Glass-Steagall, lifting the separation between commercial banks (which are federally insured) and investment firms.

While investment banks promote stocks, it is a conflict of interest for a bank to make loans to a company whose stock is being underwritten or brokered by the same bank.

The logic is that a firm in danger of collapse might be propped up with loans from the bank, which stands to profit from the sale of company stock.

Whereas Glass-Steagall required the functions of commercial and investment banking be kept separate, FSMA repealed that separation.

The new law allowed commercial banks to own investment firms engaged in unregulated trading in derivatives, with or without the involvement of hedge funds.

Banks also began participating in off-balance sheet accounting schemes, many of which were later found to be fraudulent.

In the 1990s, SEC chair Arthur Levitt criticized corporate bookkeeping as a numbers game, made possible by an unholy alliance of executives, accountants, and bankers.

Executives, accountants, and bankers, with the help of bipartisan support in Congress, became an unholy alliance because they were paid incentives to bear false witness.

Stock options were incentives to pursue conflicts of interest, by promoting inflated stock prices that had no basis in real value.

Fundamentally, shareholder value brought the pursuit of a high *share price* as a proxy for *share value*.

In the process, Wall Street took control of American business, as financial speculation took the place of expanded production.

Pension Games

In 1999, corporate lobbying efforts won a rule change from the labor department that governed the treatment of pension fund balances in corporate accounting.

The effect was to lift restrictions on withdrawals, and allow the use of pensions to finance company operations.

The impetus for the change was the enormous value of accumulated surplus in company pension plans.

For example, pension fund balances in 1999 were

- GE   - $25 Billion
- Verizon - $24 Billion
- AT&T   - $20 Billion

Lowenstein estimates roughly 10 percent of GE's reported profits were actually based on earnings from the company's employee pension fund.

Following the 1999 rule change, companies granted unprecedented benefits to executives, and reallocated pension fund surpluses to support stock prices.

By 2011, the $24 billion pension surplus at Verizon had been completely wiped out.

From 2000 to 2012, employee pension assets at GE declined by $46.7 billion dollars (from $25 billion surplus to $21.7 billion deficit).

In the same period, employee pension assets at AT&T declined $36.2 billion (from $20 billion surplus to $16.2 billion deficit).

This extraordinary decline in the value of employee pension plans reflects the use of accounting rules to report consistently higher earnings, and drive stock prices higher.

Companies also use bankruptcy as a way of shedding pensions and bringing the restructured entity back into business without the burden of employee retirement plans.

At many companies management relied on assumptions, based on the booming market of the 1990s, which showed pension obligations would be met by stock gains on the accumulated value of the fund.

This relieved the need for company contributions, until the market collapsed in the early 2000s.

For example, in 2002 United Airlines had a pension fund deficit of $10 billion dollars.

In the process of declaring bankruptcy, United was able to move that $10 billion obligation to the Pension Benefit Guaranty Corporation (PBGC).

The PBGC is a federal agency created to protect pensions.

By 2006, *more than 18,000 companies* had underfunded employee pension plans, creating a combined deficit of $450 billion dollars.

Figure 13
Pension Plan Benefits

	Plan Balance	Employee Contributions	Monthly Benefit	Interest Equivalent
Pension plan	$73,409	7% of salary	$656	10.7%
403b plan	$140,006	11% of salary	$280	2.4%

Source: Arizona state retirement system - member statement; 403b employee retirement plan - defined contribution plan statement, June 2011. For comparison see Donald G. Schmitt, 1985. "Today's pension plans: how much do they pay?," *Monthly Labor Review*, December 1985, pp. 19-25. For employees with final year's earnings of $40,000 and 30 years of service, the average monthly benefit at age 65 was $918.00. See table 1, page 20. www.bls.gov/opub/mlr/1985/12/art5full.pdf accessed 2/8/2016.

At United, bankruptcy cost employees *$3 billion* worth of pension benefits, while management was awarded $400 million of stock in the restructured company that emerged from bankruptcy.

Employees were also shifted to defined contribution 401(k) retirement plans, which pay far less in benefits than do pensions.

In the 1980s, mutual funds marketed the lower cost of 401(k) plans as a boon to companies, while stressing the higher returns on investment for employees.

But the retirement value of a 401(k) plan is typically far less than a comparable pension plan.

The reason is that pension benefits reflect more than simply interest paid on the accumulated balance.

Retirees typically choose to receive larger benefit payments during their lifetimes, instead of opting for a death benefit and smaller lifetime payments.

This option leaves a plan balance to accumulate in the pension fund, which supports the level of benefits paid to other members.

The significance is that pension plans pay benefits that are typically much higher than returns that can realistically be made from investments.

Figure 13 shows a real world case of a pension plan with an accumulated balance of $73,409, and a monthly benefit of $656.28

The 403(b) is a variant of the 401(k) designated for university employees.

In the early 1990s, the employee opted out of the pension plan in favor of a 403(b) plan.

With a much larger percentage contribution of salary allocated to the 403(b), over a 20 year period the contributions and accumulated interest grew to $140,006.

But the interest equivalent of the pension benefit is 10.73 percent.

In the second quarter 2011, the rate of return on the 403(b) was 2.4 percent.

Interest rates are much lower today than they were twenty years ago.

Interest rates aren't likely to go back up any time soon, and certainly not to anywhere near the levels of the early to mid-1990s.

Dollar for dollar, the pension benefit is worth more than 4 times the value of earnings in the 403(b).

The fundamental issue is the transfer of risk from employers to employees.

A monthly pension benefit is guaranteed for life.

In contrast, the only way to increase the monthly benefit in the 403(b) plan is to make investments with higher risk.

And yet it is clearly inappropriate to advise someone in retirement to take on more risk in hopes of generating higher returns.

Consider the percentage of private sector employees with defined benefit pension plans:

- 1980 – 83%
- 2006 – 34%
- 2011 – 15%

In the same period, participants in 401(k) plans went from 7 million in 1984, to more than 50 million in 2012.

Roughly half the assets in 401(k) plans and individual retirement accounts (IRAs) are invested in mutual funds

By 2015, the value of 401(k) assets was projected to reach $4 trillion dollars.

With half those assets invested in mutual funds, the management fees paid on mutual funds amount to some *$3 billion dollars a year.*

In exchange, employees receive monthly benefits that might be worth only 25 percent of pension benefits that were the norm for the previous generation.

Today, the widespread use of 401(k) plans essentially forces employees to use their retirement funds to gamble in the stock market.

While Wall Street has clearly benefited from the change, investment gains that once eased concerns over stagnant wages have disappeared.

The impact has been two-fold.

First, as financial profits have overtaken the level of profits from production, employees have effectively participated in their own demise.

As in every sector of society, employees were given incentives to contribute to the system of casino capitalism that has destroyed productive industry.

Second, since the transition has been made, the interests of retirees are now captive to the interests of Wall Street.

With large scale investment in the system by employees, nearly everyone now hopes for a return to the financial inflation (stock and house price inflation) that made it attractive in the first place.

This is the essence of a Ponzi scheme. Speculative booms only pay off as long as they continue to expand.

The public was persuaded to accept the financial economy as a viable substitute for the real economy.

Financialization vs. Production
In the 1980s and 1990s, the U.S. economy was restructured through a process of financial engineering.

The impact has been one of financialization, in which the financial sector has become the main driver of growth.

The parallel development has been unprecedented expansion of debt.

Easy credit fueled speculative booms, first in the stock market and then housing, because credit was used to buy stocks and houses at inflated prices.

The expansion of debt reflects deregulation of finance and increase in leverage across all sectors of the economy.

The growth of debt for non-financial business reflects financial activities, as well as LBOs that restructure companies and leave them burdened with high debt-to-equity after the value of their assets have been sold.

There is also clear evidence that corporations have increasingly used profits to buy stocks instead of making productive investments.

For example, between 1970 and 1979 non-financial firms spent $1.30 on stock investments for every $1 dollar spent on productive investment.

Twenty years later, the ratio had changed dramatically.

Between 1998 and 2007, non-financial firms spent $27 on stock trading for every $1 dollar allocated to productive investment.

At the same time, about a quarter of the amount spent on financial investments was borrowed.

These non-financial firms were not only shifting away from productive investment, but were also taking on debt to leverage investments in finance.

Speculative finance has had a corrupting influence, even for non-financial business.

It stands to reason when Wall Street was making billions through speculation, their corporate clients would see stocks as a better source of profit than investments in domestic industry.

Financial firms have become highly leveraged as they take on debt for speculative investments, but are also envied by productive industry for generating spectacular levels of profit.

At the same time, non-financial firms have become increasingly oriented toward financial profits gained through short term stock performance.

The end result has been a diversion of domestic investment away from productive industry.

The corresponding trend has been the rise in productive investment overseas, as companies shifted production to countries with low wages and minimal regulation of industry.

As offshoring allows for lower production costs, profits and stock prices have soared in tandem with the rising rate of unemployment, the declining wage share of productivity, and long term stagnation in wages.

Multinational business and financial interests are directly opposed to the interests of Americans employed in domestic industry.

This country is now in a terminal state of industrial decline, brought on by the rise of finance and the pursuit of financial profit through downsizing and offshoring of manufacturing.

Financial reform
In the early 2000s there were epic scandals in the collapse and bankruptcy of companies like Enron, Global Crossing, and World Com.

The headlines were filled with criminal prosecution of top executives and accounting firms like Arthur Anderson.

The response in 2002 was passage of a financial reform bill known as Sarbanes-Oxley.

Sarbanes-Oxley imposed disclosure requirements and created an Accounting Oversight Board to review company financial records and prevent fraudulent reporting.

And as previously mentioned, in 2004 the FASB passed its rule that requires companies to disclose the expense of stock options in their financial statements.

Essentially, Sarbanes-Oxley and the FASB rule were intended to re-assure the markets, by imposing requirements for integrity in financial reporting.

Yet, as important as these measures were, the underlying problem was never addressed.

The underlying problem is the practice of granting stock options to CEOs and other top executives.

Stock options are the corner stone of promoting *shareholder value*, because they guarantee management will pursue high stock prices.

As we've seen, this has been the mechanism whereby financial interests gained control over American business.

The process has created enormous wealth for Wall Street and U.S. multinationals, at the expense of American industry.

Stock options promote offshoring, because companies that move manufacturing overseas have larger profits, and hence higher stock values.

The logical conclusion is that executive compensation with stock options should be outlawed.

It is beyond unacceptable that offshoring is promoted by Wall Street and by CEOs who are paid hundreds of millions of dollars to move production to low wage countries.

There was also nothing in Sarbanes-Oxley that prevented collusion between the banks and the ratings agencies that created the 2008 financial crisis.

Along the same lines, there were pension reform bills passed in 2006 and 2012, which imposed audit requirements and limited what companies can do with their pension funds.

Yet, it isn't hard to see that the underlying problem wasn't addressed.

The underlying problem is that our politicians (who themselves have pensions) promote the idea that 401(k) plans are a viable alternative to a company pension.

For the overwhelming majority, the prospect of retirement based on social security and a 401(k) plan, is daunting.

It is beyond unacceptable that the public should be expected to depend on the stock market for retirement.

Pensions have been shown to be far more cost effective (lower contributions generate higher benefits), than 401(k) plans.

Private sector employees need pension plans that don't disappear every time they change jobs.

The logical conclusion is that the problem can't be left to employers to solve.

The Consumer Financial Protection Bureau (CFPB) is an independent agency responsible for consumer protection in the financial sector.

The CFPB could administer a voluntary pension plan for private sector employees who want a reliable way to build security for retirement.

While funding would be provided by contributions from both employers and employees, the current penalties faced by short term employees would be eliminated.

Pensions are designed to maximize the benefits of large pools of people participating in the plans over a long period.

Long term employment was the norm when the economy was based on manufacturing.

But today the economy is based on finance, and short term employment has become the norm.

It doesn't make sense to penalize people in the workforce for changes in the job market that are beyond their control.

Government policy has been the driving force behind the change, and the federal government should take responsibility for the problems it has played such a central role in creating.

The CFPB could administer a private employee pension plan, and give every working person the same retirement security that was the norm for the previous generation.

There is one obstacle that poses a serious challenge.

The problem is that 401(k) plans generate *$3 billion dollars a year* in fees for Wall Street.

That's why the only option available to some 70 percent of employees is the 401(k).

Between 2013 and 2014, median household income for those 65 and older declined by 2.7 percent, to just under $37,000.

As more people reach retirement age with inadequate resources in their 401(k) plans, income for that age group will go down.

With the Census Bureau reporting more than 46 million people age 65 and above, the implications for the economy are sobering.

For example, if for that age group median household income rose to $47,000, the impact would create much more demand than would median income at $37,000.

Based on 30 million households, a difference of $10,000 per household would add an additional $300 billion a year in median income.

Boosting consumer demand by some $300 billion a year would have a dramatic impact on the economy overall.

The question to consider is what value there is to the larger economy, for retirement savings in 401(k) plans to generate $3 billion a year in fees for Wall Street?

The reality is that the system currently in place creates a drag on the economy that we can't afford to ignore.

For a real economy business, profits are based on sales. But businesses can't make sales to low income households.

So if you think raising retirement income is about feeling sorry for people, you're missing the point.

The only way to create jobs is to make it profitable for real economy companies to do business in America.

The way to ensure that result is to re-establish a market of high income consumers.

The fact is, income distribution impacts the economy, and excess profits on Wall Street undermine demand.

Excess profits create millionaire incomes for a small group of people who are sucking the economy dry.

That's why SWIFT Act proposals include establishing a private employee pension system administered by the CFPB.

We can unite in common cause and insist on reform, or we can all live with the consequences of letting Wall Street run our country into the ground.

Food for Thought

Financialization has transformed the economy, as Wall Street has gained control of productive industry, and generated unprecedented profits in the stock market.

This historic transformation is a consequence of:
- anti-inflation policy,
- expansion of credit to over $50 trillion,
- deregulation of both industry and finance,
- non-regulation of new financial products,
- new accounting rules used by financial firms and non-financial business, and
- bipartisan support for the process.

Anti-inflation policy, unprecedented expansion of credit, and the absence of regulation created incentives for a new kind of growth, driven more by financial engineering than by expansion of production.

The promotion of shareholder value created an exclusive focus on stock values for non-financial firms.

The shared interest in promoting stock prices created an unholy alliance of bankers, executives, and accountants, who made billions from the destruction of American industry.

Unchecked leverage allowed Wall Street's capture of non-financial companies, and created incentive to shed large workforce lines of business.

The decline of manufacturing, through downsizing and offshoring, is the direct result of official policy, maintained in both Democratic and Republican administrations.

Main Points

The final development that completed the process of financialization was a change in the Federal Reserve's anti-inflation policy.

As *product inflation* declined in the mid-1990s, Fed policy became captive to financial interests by *supporting asset prices*.

This amounted to using low interest rates to mitigate the impact of the stock market collapse, while simultaneously creating a new boom in the housing market.

Alan Greenspan promoted the boom in housing, in part based on belief that potential speculation would be limited by high transaction costs.

Greenspan gave speeches on the virtues of adjustable rate mortgages, while refusing to crack down on predatory lending that was known to occur in refinancing.

Both Greenspan and his successor, Ben Bernanke, made public statements to the effect they anticipated interest rates to remain low for a long period.

Thereafter, between June 2004 and June 2006, the Fed raised rates 17 times in an effort to slow the explosive boom in housing.

Inflows of foreign money, which were invested in the U.S. market, kept interest rates from rising and fueled the continuing rise in stock and house prices.

When the mortgage sector collapsed, the Fed was blamed for keeping rates too low for too long, which created the boom, and then for the rate increases that finally burst the bubble.

The reality is that Fed policy became captive to the necessity of supporting asset prices, because the New Economy depends on asset price inflation for growth.

Stagnation in the real economy was offset by exponential growth of financial wealth in the form of high stock and real estate prices.

Collapse of these financial booms threatened the model of debt driven growth, which the Fed itself had created.

Boom and Bust Banking

Federal Reserve policy under Alan Greenspan spanned two distinct phases.

From his appointment in 1987 through 1996, Greenspan held to anti-inflation policy, while at the same time overseeing de-regulation (and non-regulation) of finance, as well as fostering the new system of credit without reserves.

As a percentage of disposal income, personal savings had already fallen from 10.5 percent in the early 1980s to an average 6.5 percent by the end of the decade.

Personal savings declined still further under the Greenspan Fed, to only 3.1 percent in 1999.

The decline in savings fed consumption, as did new forms of unregulated credit that made it easier to borrow.

The pursuit of anti-inflation policy was aided by the trade deficit, which helped keep inflation low with cheap imports.

The second phase began when the Fed started cutting rates despite strong economic growth and clear signs of a growing asset bubble in the stock market.

First, between July 1995 and January 1996 the Fed cut rates three times in less than a year.

Greenspan's justification was: "As a result of the monetary tightening initiated in 1994, inflationary pressures have receded enough to accommodate a modest adjustment in monetary conditions."

In reality, lower rates were one aspect of a two-part response to the Mexican peso crisis of 1995, which was then repeated after the Asian financial crisis of 1997.

With prompting from Treasury Secretary Robert Rubin, Greenspan agreed to increase liquidity as a way of offsetting the collapse of foreign markets, first in Mexico and later throughout Asia.

Increasing liquidity means expanding the money supply.

In 1995 and 1996, the money supply expanded at nearly five times the rate of the preceding 1990 – 1994 period.

This increased liquidity was the context in which the Dow Jones Industrial average rose from 4,000 in early 1995 to over 6,000 in 1996, *a gain of more than 50 percent.*

In 1997, the money supply grew even faster, expanding by $465 billion dollars.

Remarkably, this accelerated rate of money growth was accompanied by a fall in the rate of inflation.

Recall that the basis for nearly doubling interest rates between January 1994 and February 1995 was the fear that falling unemployment might be inflationary.

Yet while the economy surged with GDP growth at 4 percent in 1996, inflation fell below 3 percent in 1997, and then below 2 percent in 1998.

After 1997, Greenspan saw no reason to hold rates at levels some four percent higher than the rate of inflation.

At the May 1998 meeting of the Federal Open Market Committee (FOMC), which is responsible for setting interest rates, Greenspan was warned that the continuing rise in stock prices would eventually collapse.

His response was definitive:
"I have concluded that in the broader sense we have to stay with our fundamental central bank goal, namely, to stabilize product price levels."

Later that year, the collapse of the Russian ruble brought the fall of Long Term Capital Management (LTCM), which was a Wall Street hedge fund heavily invested in the Russian bond market.

Thereafter, the Fed lowered interest rates three times in three months in the fall of 1998, essentially as a means of reassuring the markets.

The market value of stocks on the New York Stock Exchange then rose from $9 trillion in June 1998 to $12.6 trillion in June 1999, *a 40 percent increase*.

In the same 12 month period, the market value of NASDAQ stocks rose from $1.7 trillion to $3.2 trillion, *an increase of 90 percent*.

Prior to the 1929 crash, the total value of stocks was around 85 percent of GDP.

In 1999, stock values rose to a level just under 179 percent of GDP.

Greenspan's insistence on the goal of stabilizing *product* price levels, and not *asset* price levels, had become the guiding premise behind boom and bust banking.

Product prices are reflected in the wholesale price index, which uses the cost of a sample basket of goods to determine average prices that producers receive for their output.

This index of wholesale prices is the oldest measure of what is generally understood as the rate of inflation.

Greenspan used interest rates to control inflation by controlling product prices.

But he was ambivalent about trying to control asset prices, such as stock prices.

Instead, he promoted the boom as reflecting legitimate values for stocks, which were being driven higher by rising productivity.

In 1998 Greenspan delivered a speech on the emergence of a New Economy, in which rising productivity could spur economic growth without the onset of inflation.

The economy did in fact benefit from developments that were driving growth, while also creating downward pressure on inflation.

First, productivity growth rose substantially in the mid-1990s, and then grew at an average annual rate of 3 percent between 1996 and 2004.

The surge marked the first sustained growth in productivity since the 1970s, and was more than twice the average 1.4 percent rate that prevailed from 1974 to 1995.

The cause was a dramatic reduction in computer costs, and the mass market that emerged despite modest growth in wages.

As processing power grew while prices fell, the cost of computer power fell by more than 30 percent per year in the second half of the 1990s.

The impact was to create a mass market for computer products that generated enormous profits through economies of scale.

Matching the fall in computing cost, sales of personal computers and investment in information technologies (internet and software) both grew more than 30 percent per year in the late 1990s.

These products were highly standardized (PC or Mac), but could also support customized applications for a wide variety of end users.

This meant computer technology developed in a way that minimized the fragmentation of consumer markets that served to undermine productivity in the 1970s.

At the same time, wage increases were modest compared to the marked increase in productivity.

Second, following U.S. victory in the Gulf War against Iraq in 1991, the price of oil declined thereafter for eight consecutive years, reaching a record low of $11.91 per barrel in 1998.

After adjusting for inflation, the oil price per barrel was 40 percent lower in 1998 than it was in 1972.

Thus, rising productivity without a comparable rise in wages, combined with record low oil prices, created an environment of strong growth without inflation.

"Leaning into the wind" describes policy that is pro-cyclical.

See the appendix for discussion of pro-cyclical and counter-cyclical policy.

Third, devaluation of foreign currencies drove up the value of the dollar, and created a flood of both
- cheap imports from low wage countries, and
- foreign money entering the U.S. market

The first of these started with the Mexican debt crisis, which led to a 70 percent devaluation of the peso in 1995.

This brought a U.S. trade deficit with Mexico of nearly $16 billion in 1995 and $17.5 billion in 1996, with a corresponding flow of Mexican investments into dollar denominated assets.

These investments drove up stock prices in the initial 1995/96 boom, although the value of financial flows from the peso crisis was dwarfed by those stemming from the Asian crisis that followed.

In 1997 the Asian financial crisis resulted in devaluations for South Korea, Thailand, and Indonesia.

Between 1997 and 2000, the U.S. trade deficit with Pacific Rim countries (not including China) grew by more than $100 billion dollars.

This brought $100 billion worth of cheap imports into the U.S. market, which kept inflation from rising.

At the same time, $100 billion of foreign investments in dollar denominated assets entered the U.S. credit market, and drove up stock prices even further.

The response from the Federal Reserve was to lower rates, *because Greenspan viewed interest rates purely in terms of product inflation.*

The Fed chairman had been using high interest rates as anti-inflation policy for nine years.

When inflation fell below 3 percent in 1997 and below 2 percent in 1998, Greenspan cut rates because he saw no justification for keeping rates higher.

This move amounted to "leaning into the wind," or using interest rates to push the economy further in the direction it was already moving.

At the same time, Greenspan refused to raise margin requirements on stock trading.

Based on blind faith in the efficiency of markets, the Fed chairman testified before Congress that raising margin requirements would create distortions in the natural functioning of the stock exchange.

Greenspan also argued there was no way to identify a "bubble" until after it burst.

"To spot a bubble in advance requires a judgment that hundreds of thousands of informed investors have it all wrong."

His conclusion was that the Fed should take aggressive action only after the fact, typically by reducing rates when a collapse in one sector poses a threat to the wider economy.

This was a revealing juncture, because Greenspan made specific reference to providing liquidity after the 1987 stock market crash, as well as to lowering rates and continuing to provide liquidity after the 1998 collapse of LTCM.

This policy of reluctance to prevent bubbles from forming, and intervening only after the fact, became known as the Greenspan "put."

The owner of a "put" option has the option to sell a stock or bond at a pre-determined price.

The effect is to provide a floor on the value of the asset, which limits potential losses.

Greenspan's "put" was the commitment of the Federal Reserve to intervene and limit the losses caused by periodic collapse of the markets.

This meant the Fed had adopted the role of engineering the economy in ways designed to protect financial profits.

In June 1999 unemployment had reached a 30 year low of 4 percent, while stock trading had reached record highs.

Earlier in the year, long term interest rates on U.S. Treasury bonds, which were set by traders in the sovereign bond markets, began rising.

In response the Fed raised rates in quarter point increments, from 4.75 percent in early 1999, to 5.5 percent in November of that year.

These moves had no impact on the stock market, and were criticized for being virtually meaningless.

The reason was the context in which these minimal rate increases were made.

From the beginning of 1998 through the end of 1999, the Fed expanded the money supply by over $1 trillion dollars.

This included the injection of $50 billion of liquidity provided to banks, designed to offset any potential impact of crossing the threshold to the year 2000.

This much feared Y2K problem centered on the idea that computers would be unable to change the date to a year ending in zeros, which could wreak havoc in the financial sector.

These moves by the Fed brought an expansion of lending, while low import prices kept inflation from rising.

The combined impact of low interest rates, the Fed's expansion of the money supply, and financial inflows from foreign sources, was to feed what was already an unprecedented boom in the stock market.

In 2000 the Fed continued raising rates, to a high of 6.5 per cent.

The higher rates coincided with the rise in oil prices to $27 per barrel, and with the bursting of the dot.com bubble.

The NASDAQ stock exchange, on which tech stocks were traded, closed at 5,048 on March 10th, 2000.

Within 18 months, the NASDAQ had fallen to 1,114, losing nearly 80 percent of its value, equivalent to roughly $5 trillion of equity.

In the interim, the country was struck by the terrorist attacks of September 2001.

With the steep decline in travel that followed, there was a sharp fall in consumer spending.

As the economy stalled, Greenspan became concerned about the possible onset of *deflation*, if something wasn't done to stimulate demand.

The Fed then lowered rates dramatically, from 6.5 percent in 2000 to 1 percent by August 2003, and successfully mitigated what might otherwise have been a severe recession.

Unfortunately, this method of minimizing recession created a new boom in the housing sector, which Greenspan intentionally engineered and encouraged as it developed.

Greenspan argued the only way to prevent the onset of deflation was to lower interest rates to 1 percent.

His belief was that extremely low interest rates would create a housing boom, but without creating a speculative bubble.

In a 2003 speech the Fed chairman described the housing market as being unlike stock markets, in that high transaction costs in the housing sector made it virtually immune to speculation.

But this ignored the widespread practice of "originate to distribute," in which mortgages were originated and then packaged as securities and sold to Wall Street investment firms.

Extremely low interest rates between 2001 and 2004 fueled the housing boom, while Greenspan provided commentary to sustain it.

For example, of particular concern at the time was the upsurge in adjustable rate mortgages (ARMs).

Greenspan praised the increase in ARMs in 2004, because "Many homeowners might have saved tens of thousands of dollars" by converting a fixed rate mortgage to an ARM that offered a low initial rate.

Both Greenspan and Board of Governors member Ben Bernanke also made explicit statements to the effect they anticipated rates would remain low over a long period.

These statements effectively endorsed the practice, which put millions of homeowners at risk once interest rates began to rise.

In mid-2004 Greenspan once again began raising rates.

Between 2004 and 2006 the Fed raised rates to 5.25 percent on federal funds it loans to banks, in an effort to slow the boom in the housing market.

But there was virtually no impact on the boom, because the unprecedented expansion of credit had by that point undermined the Fed's ability to control the economy.

What Fed chairman Alan Greenspan failed to appreciate was the inherent danger posed by
- the system of creating credit without reserves,
- the virtual absence of financial regulation, and
- the influx of foreign capital caused by trade deficits

Instead, Greenspan had complete faith in the sanctity of self-regulating markets.

In 1998, Greenspan made a revealing statement during the fight over exempting derivatives from regulation.

In an exchange with CFTC chair Brooksley Born, Greenspan said:
"…you probably will always believe there should be laws against fraud, and I don't think there is any need for a law against fraud."

Greenspan's view was that derivatives dealers who might commit fraud would be discovered, and that their clients would stop doing business with them.

In 2004, the SEC made a similar show of deference to self-regulating markets with its *net capital exemption rule*, which reduced capital requirements for Wall Street brokerage firms.

The exemption rule allowed investment banks to adopt *their own guidelines* for assessing the value of the bank's capital considered to be at risk.

Thereafter, debt-to-equity ratios rose from 15-to-1 in 2004, to more than 30-to-1 in 2008.

In the span of 20 years, belief in efficient markets revolutionized thinking about the economy, and endorsed speculative finance as the ultimate engine of growth.

What is relevant today is the observation made by Keynes in the depths of the Great Depression:
"Speculators may do no harm as bubbles on a steady stream of enterprise, but when enterprise becomes the bubble on a whirlpool of speculation, the job of capitalism is likely to be ill-done."

Financialization of the economy has created precisely this situation, in which enterprise—what we call productive industry—has become the bubble on a whirlpool of Wall Street speculation.

The contrast between Keynes and former Treasury secretary Larry Summers goes to the heart of the issue.

In 1997, Summers was quoted in the Wall Street Journal as saying:
"Financial markets don't just oil the wheels of economic growth—they *are* the wheels."

The advent of unregulated finance, fueled further by low interest rates, created massive speculation and unprecedented growth of credit that now defines the parameters of the system.

These were the conditions that led to the perfect storm of 2008, and these same conditions have been perpetuated in the Great Recession that continues today.

Food for Thought

In the mid-1990s, Alan Greenspan's exclusive focus on preventing *product inflation* gave legitimacy to the rise of *asset price inflation*.

The new policy framework of accepting trade deficits as legitimate, and expanded access to credit in financial markets, transformed the economy.

The New Economy is characterized by
- an overvalued U.S. dollar
- unprecedented trade deficits
- product price inflation near zero
- unprecedented asset price inflation
- decline of manufacturing industry
- decoupling of productivity and wages
- decline of the economy's capacity to create jobs
- slow and distorted growth: with a growth rate of 2 percent since 2012, the economy is growing 40 percent more slowly than the historic average, and has accumulated $15 trillion in lost production value.
- unprecedented expansion of credit market debt, to more than $55 trillion dollars

The foundations of the New Economy are
- cheap imports,
- debt financed consumption, and
- financial booms based on inflated asset prices

These fundamentals of the New Economy are no different today than before the 2008 financial crisis.

Economic fundamentals haven't changed, because the primary response to the 2008 financial crisis has been renewed support for asset prices.

In 2008 – 2009, an unprecedented $7.7 trillion dollars was allocated to bailouts and federal loan guarantees.

Thereafter, Fed chairman Ben Bernanke and Treasury secretary Tim Geithner made a series of deals to purchase toxic assets from Wall Street banks.

The impact has been to provide continuing support for asset prices.

The stock market is posting record highs, while house prices in most markets are again rising.

Public commentary seems to support the idea that *prices before the 2008 collapse were normal*, instead of recognizing the extraordinary inflation of house prices that ultimately crashed.

What is lacking is meaningful discussion of what will be required to restore the process of wealth creation in the real economy.

Instead, the policy focus continues, virtually unchanged, based on failure to recognize the New Economy as a failed paradigm.

Quotes on Banks

"If ever again our nation stumbles upon unfunded paper, it shall surely be like death to our body politic. This country will crash."

George Washington

"Banks have done more injury to the religion, morality, tranquility, prosperity, and even wealth of the nation than they…ever will do good."

John Adams

"I believe that banking institutions are more dangerous to our liberties than standing armies."

Thomas Jefferson

"History records that the money changers have used every form of abuse, intrigue, deceit, and violent means possible to maintain their control over governments by controlling money and its issuance."

James Madison

"The banking powers are more despotic than a monarchy…They denounce as public enemies all who question their methods or throw light upon their crimes."

"…the money power of the country will endeavor to prolong its reign by working upon the prejudices of the people until all wealth is aggregated in a few hands, and the Republic is destroyed."

Abraham Lincoln

"Our great industrial nation is controlled by its system of credit. Therefore all of our activities are in the hands of a small group of men who chill and check true economic freedom."

Woodrow Wilson

"The one aim of these financiers is world control by the creation of inextinguishable debt."

"It is well enough that people of the nation do not understand our banking and monetary system, for if they did, I believe there would be a revolution before tomorrow morning."

Henry Ford

"The real truth of the matter is…that a financial element in the large centers has owned the government ever since the days of Andrew Jackson."

Franklin D. Roosevelt

"And the banks - hard to believe in a time when we're facing a banking crisis that many of the banks created - are still the most powerful lobby on Capitol Hill. And they frankly own the place."

Richard Durbin

"Rather than justice for all, we are evolving into a system of justice for those who can afford it. We have banks that are not only too big to fail, but too big to be held accountable."

Joseph Stiglitz

Summary

The New Economy destroyed the circle of growth, which was based on full employment and wage increases tied to rising productivity.

In the circle of growth, rising wages lead to higher demand and full employment.

In turn, high demand and full employment create incentive for productive investment, spurring gains in productivity, higher wages, and a reinforcing spiral of growth.

The New Economy was born when the goal of full employment was abandoned as inflationary.

The ultimate result was to sever the link between productivity and wages.

First, economic policy aimed at generating high growth was replaced by anti-inflation policy.

This meant deregulation of industry to promote cost cutting, as well as reliance on trade deficits to provide cheap imports to consumers.

Second, financial deregulation allowed the use of innovative products designed to increase leverage and expand the availability of equity that could be used for collateral.

The combined result was that stagnation in the real economy was offset by cheap imports and asset price inflation in the financial economy.

House and stock price inflation helped maintain political support, with the promise of creating wealth based on real estate and high returns in the stock market.

Demand previously driven by wage growth was replaced with demand driven by debt and by inflated asset values in stock and house prices.

These features created persistent trends that include rising inequality, decoupling of wages and productivity, declining wages, slow growth, and the economy's declining capacity to create jobs.

The corresponding development was a change in policy attitudes toward the trade deficit.

Prior to the 1980s, trade deficits were recognized as representing a potential source of demand leakage through spending on imports.

In the New Economy, trade deficits bring foreign investment flowing into the country, making it possible to finance budget deficits without raising taxes.

This change represents the final component of the New Economy model of growth, based on new terms of engagement with the world economy that have transformed the global system.

The evidence for extraordinary bipartisan commitment to the New Economy is seen in Greenspan's multiple re-appointments by George H.W. Bush, Bill Clinton, and George W. Bush.

Greenspan served an unprecedented five terms as chairman of the Federal Reserve, from 1987 to 2006.

After Greenspan stepped down, the 2008 financial crisis and collapse of the housing market brought questions about unregulated finance, but not about the underlying assumptions of the New Economy.

The aftermath of the financial crisis revealed an economy that has been stripped of productive capacity, and is now unable to create the jobs needed to restore growth.

While the New Economy model is intellectually bankrupt, political debate has failed to address the underlying structural problems that set the stage for the recent crisis.

Instead, the financial sector continues to dominate the economy, while political discussion centers on the need to balance the budget.

There is rarely any mention of the kinds of reforms we need to prioritize the economic fundamentals that generate growth.

Volume III - Preview

<u>Trade Deficits and Offshoring</u>
Another revolutionary change in economic policy came with the unprecedented view that trade deficits are harmless.

The key development was the discovery that the U.S. government could run budget deficits without the economic consequences of inflation.

Historically, government deficits had been found to "crowd out" the private sector.

This means government borrowing could absorb so much money that the demand for money would go up, causing inflation.

In the mid-1980s it seemed miraculous that in spite of large budget deficits, there was no shortage of capital, and hence no inflationary impact.

This came about because the balance of payments system works differently for the U.S. than for any other country in the world.

The international reserve currency is the U.S. dollar, because oil and most other commodities are paid for in dollars.

When another country runs a trade surplus, it has to buy dollar denominated assets to invest that surplus.

For this reason, the U.S. trade deficit is offset by money coming into the country, called financial inflows.

These inflows allow the U.S. to finance budget deficits using foreign capital, which eliminates the need to raise taxes.

The significance is that the federal government can run budget deficits, year in and year out, without those deficits causing inflation.

When budget deficits can be financed without inflation, there are no short term consequences.

As a result, there is no incentive to make the politically unpopular move of raising taxes to balance the budget.

Presidents from Reagan to Obama have run the country through this twin deficit system, by financing deficits with the sale of dollar assets to trade surplus countries.

This use of foreign money to finance the budget gives politicians a vested interest in supporting trade deficits.

The extraordinary consequence is that offshoring is discussed in terms of the benefits of free trade, instead of the loss of high wage jobs in manufacturing.

Suppose any future president wants to reverse the loss of manufacturing and reduce the trade deficit.

That president would have to explain why raising taxes would be required to finance the budget.

Why?

Because a lower trade deficit would reduce financial inflows, and thereby limit the ability to run our government using foreign money to finance the budget.

This dependence on foreign capital to finance the budget makes the U.S. vulnerable to foreign governments.

For example, with the bulk of financial inflows originating in China, the Chinese government has accumulated some $2 trillion dollars in U.S. treasury bonds.

The U.S. walks a fine line with complaints about China's currency manipulation, because we sell bonds to China to finance the federal budget.

At the same time, the influx of foreign money provides cover to discussion of offshoring as being synonymous with free trade.

In fact, offshoring is not trade.

"Trade" refers to the sale of things we make in this country, to other countries—and vice versa.

In contrast, offshoring refers to
- shutting down productive capability in this country,
- re-building that capability offshore, and
- selling things made offshore, back into the American market.

As a case in point, roughly half of U.S. imports from China are actually made by American companies with offshore production in China.

Paul Craig Roberts served as Assistant Secretary of the Treasury in the Reagan administration, and has long been an outspoken critic of offshoring.

To paraphrase Roberts, there is nothing in economic theory that says a country benefits from moving its productive capability offshore.

There's also nothing in "free trade" theory that addresses the extraordinary commitment by China to provide incentives for U.S. companies to offshore production.

Along with access to low wage labor, American companies in China benefit from export subsidies and a currency undervalued by an estimated 40 percent relative to the dollar.

Officials in the U.S. Treasury have also orchestrated currency devaluation for other low wage countries throughout Asia.

The reality is that official policy favors Wall Street financial interests and U.S. multinationals that profit from offshoring.

This *Wall Street / Trade complex* controls trade policy, and profits from low wage labor and high stock prices for companies with offshore production.

These are the issues SWIFT Act proposals are designed to address.

SWIFT Action for Permanent Recovery

SWIFT Act proposals are revenue neutral, and are based on 5 core principles.

Smart Growth

Permanent recovery can only be achieved through revival of the real economy, led by manufacturing and high technology, high-value-added industries.

Recovery will also require reducing the trade deficit and reforming the financial sector to fundamentally restructure the national economy.

The economy's capacity to create wealth and jobs has declined, because investments that should have been made in productive industry have been used instead for speculative finance or foreign investment.

The country now faces multiple deficits (the federal budget deficit, public investment deficit, private investment deficit, and the trade deficit), which any plan for recovery has to address.

Without slow and distorted growth, there would be no budget deficits.

The goal of Smart Growth reflects acknowledgement that permanent recovery will require economic restructuring.

Wage Standards

Imposing wage standards on imports will prohibit unfair wage competition and reduce offshoring.

American industry can't compete with cheap imports, often made with wages between 50 cents and $1 an hour, and to some extent with child labor.

Even so, higher wages in the export sectors of poor countries would have limited impact on prices in the American market.

Corporations can't raise prices without losing sales, because consumers no longer have the income or even the credit to pay higher prices.

Instead, higher wages overseas would raise global demand for U.S. exports.

Increasing U.S. exports would reduce unemployment and spur growth in this country.

The result would be higher demand, in both the U.S. and abroad, which would increase sales and drive economic growth around the world.

Industrial Policy

Strategic promotion of manufacturing and advanced technology industry is critical to U.S. competitiveness in world markets.

Consider that between 1995 and 2010, the U.S. traded places with China in a wide range of manufacturing industries.

In 1995, the U.S. out-produced China 7 to 1 in low, medium, and high technology industries.

But in 2010, China out-produced the U.S. in every category, and by nearly 2 to 1 in medium technology industries.

American industry can't compete with producers that have the support of foreign governments.

Large scale investments in high technology industry are essential to
- support the demand generating process, and
- re-establish the virtuous circle of growth.

What is needed is beyond argument.

But there isn't enough demand in the economy to justify private sector investment.

Without publicly funded investments, the U.S. economy will continue to unravel.
.

Financial Reform

Unprecedented growth of the financial sector has reduced incentive for productive investment and diminished the economy's capacity to create jobs.

At the same time, Wall Street interests and too-big-to-fail banks have successfully lobbied to block meaningful reform.

SWIFT Act proposals address five essential areas of financial reform:

First, reduce systemic risk, by
- requiring separation between commercial banks and investment firms, and
- imposing size limitations to break up the banks and prevent future bailouts, and
- setting limits on the use of leverage throughout the system

Regulatory exemptions for trading in derivatives and foreign currency should also be repealed.

Second, the financial sector should be subject to taxes designed to establish parity between returns from financial investment and the investments needed in productive industry.

There is no chance of restoring productive investment in American industry, without addressing the excess profits generated by financial investment.

Substantial revenue can be generated by a tax of 0.05 percent (one half of one percent) on financial transactions.

That revenue could be used to fund investments in advanced technology industry.

Third, compensating corporate executives with stock options should be outlawed.

No development has done more harm to American industry than the practice of granting stock options to CEOs and other executives.

Defining corporate value in terms of short term stock prices has only served to give Wall Street financial interests leverage over productive lines of business.

CEOs have been paid to downsize operations through layoffs, and to offshore production to low wage countries.

The goal in either case is to maximize profits, and thereby maximize the short term value of company stock.

CEOs have earned hundreds of millions of dollars through stock options, while American industry has been dismantled and sent offshore.

Fourth, the Consumer Financial Protection Bureau should establish a voluntary pension plan for private sector employees.

Today the only option available to some 70 percent of employees is the 401(k), which provides far less benefit for the same contribution as a pension plan.

While 401(k) plans generate $3 billion a year in fees for Wall Street, low retirement income creates a drag on the economy overall.

The fifth area of financial reform is repeal of the Citizens United ruling that allows unlimited contributions to political campaigns.

Politicians of both parties represent the interests of Wall Street banks and U.S. multinationals with offshore production.

Such has been the corrupting influence of money in politics.

It is sheer nonsense to allow unlimited contributions, which are used to perpetuate Wall Street influence in politics.

Trade and Tax Reform
Unrestricted trade has undermined the U.S. economy and diminished the productive capacity of American industry.

A U.S. VAT would tax imports but not exports in the same way the VAT is used in over 150 countries around the world.

A VAT would make exports more profitable and imports less profitable.

The effect would be to create incentive for investment in manufacturing, and disincentive for offshoring.

Notes

Impact of Ideas

New Economy Facts and Figures

Decoupling of
Productivity and Wages
Lawrence Mishel and Kar-Fai Gee, "Why Aren't Workers Benefitting from Labor Productivity Growth in the United States?" *International Productivity Monitor*, No. 23, Spring 2012.

Slow and Distorted Growth
Jeff Madrick, 1995. *The End of Affluence: The Causes and Consequences of America's Economic Dilemma.* (New York: Random House); Robert J. Gordon, 2008,"The Slowest Potential Output Growth in U.S. History: Measurement and Interpretation," Northwestern University and National Bureau of Economic Research, paper presented as CSIP Symposium on "The Outlook for Future Productivity Growth," Federal Reserve Bank of San Francisco.

Decoupling of
GDP Growth and Employment:
Laura D'Andrea Tyson, "Jobs Deficit, Investment Deficit, Fiscal Deficit," The New York Times, Economix, July 29, 2011.

Logic of the New Economy

Anti-inflation Policy:
For impact of inflation on profitability of industry and financial sectors: Thomas I. Palley, 1998. *Plenty of Nothing: The Downsizing of the American Dream and the Case for Structural Keynsianism.* (Princeton, NJ: Princeton University Press): 119-20; Jeff Madrick, 2014. *Seven Bad Ideas: How Mainstream Economists Have Damaged America and the World.* (New York: Alfred A. Knopf): Chapter 4: 116-137.

For structure of Federal Reserve see Ibid. 122. Paul Volcker outvoted: Jeff Madrick, 2011. *Age of Greed: The Triumph of Finance and the Decline of America, 1970 to the Present.* (New York: Alfred A. Knopf): 174, and Robert Kuttner, 2007. *The Squandering of America: How the Failure of Our Politics Undermines Our Prosperity.* (New York: Vintage Books): 103.

For discussion of Greenspan in the context of Volcker's legacy: Madrick, *Age of Greed*: 232.

For Greenspan's logic behind raising rates: Palley, *Plenty of Nothing:* 111-112. For discussion of Natural Rate of Unemployment: Ibid: 108-110.

Debt Driven Growth
For description of demand gap: Thomas I. Palley, 2012. *From Financial Crisis to Stagnation: The Destruction of Shared Prosperity and the Role of Economics.* (Cambridge: Cambridge University Press): 58-59 and 146.

For system of credit without reserves: Richard Duncan, 2009. *The Corruption of Capitalism: A Strategy to Rebalance the Global Economy and Restore Sustainable Growth.* (Hong Kong: CLSA Books): 5 & 9.

For application of same standards to new forms of credit: Ibid: 5 and 12-13.

For impact of financial inflows: Ibid: 15-28. For consequential creation of service economy: Ibid: 41-45.

For further reading: Costas Lapavitsas, 2013. *Profiting Without Producing: How Finance Exploits Us All*. (New York: Verso Press).

Wall Street Rules

Financial Deregulation
Simon Johnson and James Kwak, 2010. *13 Bankers: The Wall Street Takeover and the Next Financial Meltdown*. (New York: Vintage Books): 72-74; Kuttner, *Squandering of America*: 94-105; Charles P. Kindleberger and Robert Aliber, 2005. *Manias, Panics, and Crashes: A History of Financial Crises*. Fifth Edition. (Hoboken, NJ: John Wiley & Sons): 172–175.

For the takeover movement: John Brooks, 1987. *The Takeover Game: The Men, the Moves, and the Wall Street Money Behind Today's Nationwide Merger Wars*. (New York: Truman Talley Books).

For the case of Safeway: Karen Ho, 2009. *Liquidated: An Ethnography of Wall Street*. (Durham, NC: Duke University Press): 137 150.

Share Holder Value
Allan A. Kennedy, 2000. *The End of Shareholder Value: Corporations at the Crossroads*. (Cambridge: Perseus Publishing): 49-63 specific to GE; Thomas F. O'Boyle, 1998. *At Any Cost: Jack Welch, General Electric, and the Pursuit of Profit*. (New York: Alfred A. Knopf): case study of GE; Lynn Stout, 2012. *The ShareHolder Value Myth: How Putting Shareholders First Harms Investors, Corporations, and the Public*. (San Francisco, CA: Berrett-Koehler Publishers): 63-73; and Roger L. Martin, 2011. *Fixing the Game: Bubbles, Crashes, and What Capitalism Can Learn From the NFL*. (Boston: Harvard Business Review Press).

See also William Lazonick and Mary O'Sullivan, "Maximizing shareholder value: a new ideology for corporate governance", *Economy and Society*, Volume 29 No. 1, February 2000: 13-35; Neil Fligstein and Tack-Jin Shin, "Shareholder Value and Changes in American Industries, 1984-2000." Unpublished paper, Department of Sociology, University of California, Berkeley, CA, February 2005.

Executive Compensation
Roger Lowenstein. 2004. *Origins of the Crash: The Great Bubble and Its Undoing*. (New York: Penguin Press): 35-54.

For the proposed FASB rule in 1993 and lobbying fight that followed: Ibid: 44-46.

Derivatives and <u>Mark to Model</u> Accounting
Edward LiPuma and Benjamin Lee. 2004. *Financial Derivatives and the Globalization of Risk*. (Durham, NC: Duke University Press): 33-35.

Derivatives and Enron:
Robert Scheer, 2010. *The Great American Stickup: How Reagan Republicans and Clinton Democrats Enriched Wall Street While Mugging Main Street*. (New York: Nation Books): 111-138; Lowenstein, *Origins of the Crash*. Chapter 7: 127-155, and Kindleberger and Aliber, *Manias, Panics, and Crashes*: 176-179.

Creative accounting and the impact of repealing Glass-Steagall: Joseph E. Stiglitz, 2003. *The Roaring Nineties*. (New York: W.W. Norton). Chapter 5: 115-139 and Chapter 6: 140-169, and Lowenstein, *Origins of the Crash*. Chapter 4: 55-78, and Chapter 5: 79-100.

The Dot.Com and Telecom Booms
Lowenstein, *Origins of the Crash*. Chapter 6: 101-126.

Pension Games:
Ellen E. Schultz. 2011. *Retirement Heist: How Companies Plunder and Profit From the Nest Eggs of American Workers*. (New York: Penguin Group); Kuttner, *Squandering of America:* 103.

Boom and Bust Banking

Overview of Fed Policy:
Lawrence H. White, "Monetary Policy and the Financial Crisis," in David Beckworth, ed. 2012: *Boom and Bust Banking: The Causes and Cures of the Great Recession*. (Oakland, CA: The Independent Institute): 13-26.

Boom and bust stock market values: Kindleberger and Aliber, *Manias, Panics, and Crashes:* 162-164; Madrick, *Age of Greed:* 242; Clyde Prestowitz. 2010. *The Betrayal of American Prosperity: Free Market Delusions, America's Decline, and How We Must Compete in the Post-Dollar Era*. (New York: Free Press): 122 and 130-131.

See www.indexmundi.com for the market value of U.S. stocks, which reached 178.85% of GDP in 1999.

For Greenspan's justification for cutting rates in 1995: Federal Reserve Release, July 6, 1995: http://www.federalreserve.gov

Explosion in margin debt:
Peter Hartcher. 2006. *Bubble Man: Alan Greenspan and the Missing 7 Trillion Dollars*. (New York: W.W. Norton): 136-137.

Between the end of 1995 and February 2000, margin debt more than tripled, to $265 Billion. See William A. Fleckenstein and Frederick Sheehan, 2008. *Greenspan's Bubbles: The Age of Ignorance at the Federal Reserve*. (New York: McGraw-Hill): 87. As a proportion of GDP, margin debt was at the highest level since 1929.

Greenspan quote on stabilizing product prices:
Frederick Sheehan. 2010. *Panderer To Power: The Untold Story of How Alan Greenspan Enriched Wall Street and Left a Legacy of Recession*. (New York: McGraw-Hill): 177: Quote is from *FOMC meeting transcript*, May 19, 1998: 85.

New Economy impact on Fed Policy:
Madrick, *Age of Greed*: 232-247.

Devaluation of foreign currencies:
Duncan, *Corruption of Capitalism*: 98-103

Greenspan quote on spotting a bubble:
Fleckenstein and Sheehan, *Greenspan's Bubbles*: 68:

Expansion of the money supply:
Peter Hartcher, *Bubble Man:* 132-133; Fleckenstein and Sheehan, *Greenspan's Bubbles:* 74.

See the table on expansion of the M3, which was later dropped as a metric of data gathering.

Greenspan quote on adjustable rate mortgages:
Mark Zandi, 2009. *Financial Shock: A 360 Degree Look at the Subprime Mortgage Implosion, and How to Avoid the Next Financial Crisis*. (Upper Saddle River, NJ: FT Press): 72-73.

Inflows of foreign capital:
Richard Duncan. 2012. *The New Depression: The Breakdown of the Paper Money Economy*. (Singapore: John Wiley & Sons): 24-28.

Greenspan quote on fraud:
Scheer, *Great American Stickup:* 99. Quote is from Rick Schmitt, "Prophet and Loss," *Stanford Magazine*, (April/March 2009).

Keynes quote on speculation:
John Maynard Keynes, 1964. *The General Theory of Employment, Interest and Money*. (New York: Harcourt): 159.

Larry Summers quote on role of finance:
Philip Mirowski. 2013. *Never Let a Serious Crisis Go to Waste: How Neoliberalism Survived the Financial Meltdown*. (New York: Verso): 222. Quote is from *Wall Street Journal*, December 8, 1997.

APPENDIX

Managing the Economy

Put a teapot on the stove, and turn on the flame to heat the water.

When the water is hot enough, steam comes out of the spout and makes a loud whistling sound that lets you know the water is boiling.

At that point, you should
    A) Turn the flame down, or
    B) Turn the flame up

If you chose A) Turn the flame down, you already understand the logic of counter-cyclical economic policy.

Turning the flame down reduces the heat so the water doesn't boil over.

Economic policy is either contractive (turning the flame down), or expansive (turning the flame up).

Policy makers are responsible for evaluating how hot the economy is when the decision is made to go one direction or the other.

The sections that follow explain a variety of policy tools and how they impact the economy.

Appendix Figure 1
Contractive Policy

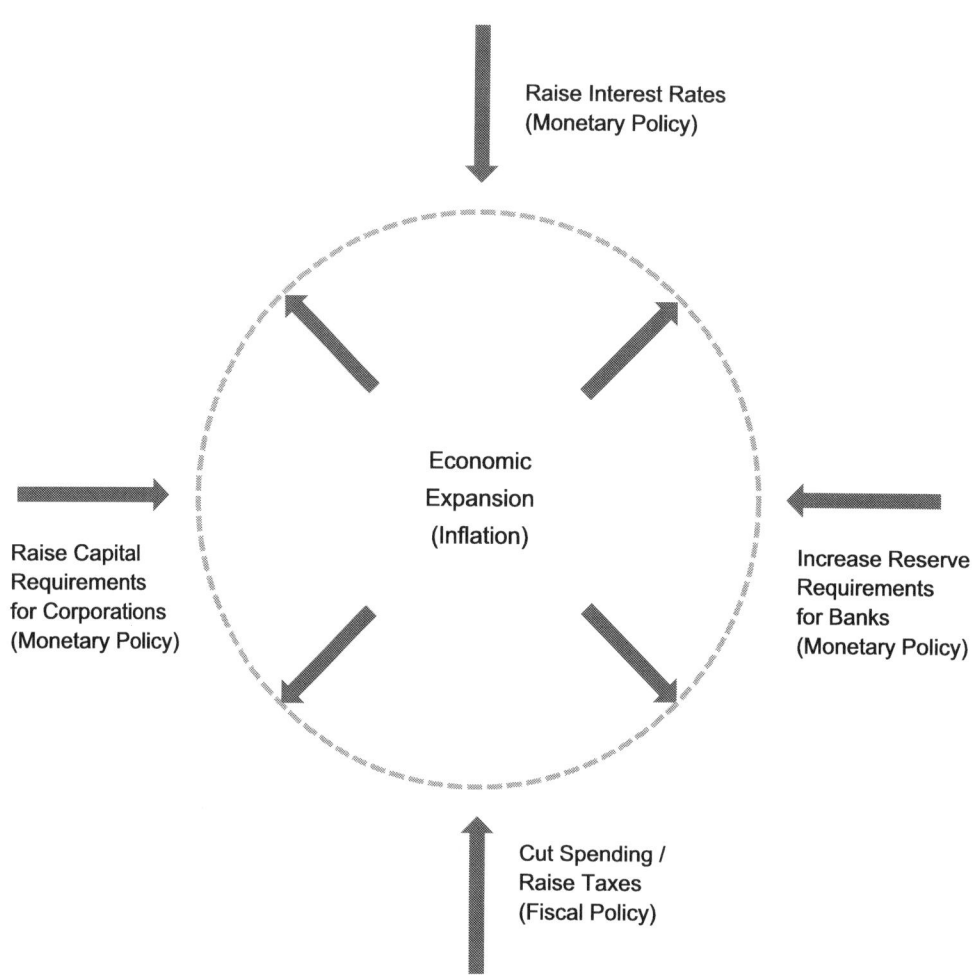

Contractive Policy

At any given point in time, the economy is either shrinking or growing.

When business is booming and sales are up, hiring accelerates, wages go up, and prices also tend to rise.

This creates inflation, and works to increase the rate of growth in a period of expansion.

When the business cycle is expansive, logic dictates the use of *contractive policy* to offset the upturn in the business cycle.

Such a period of economic expansion is shown in Figure 1, with the economy represented by the area inside the circle.

Arrows pointing outward indicate expansion of the economy.

Arrows outside the circle point inward, and represent *contractive policy tools* used to offset the upturn in the business cycle.

The Federal Reserve uses *monetary policy* to manage the availability and cost of money and credit, by controlling interest rates and the quantity of money in circulation.

Monetary policy is contractive when interest rates are raised, and/or
- reserve requirements for banks are raised,
- capital requirements for corporations are raised.

Raising reserve requirements forces banks to set aside more cash in reserve relative to loans.

Raising capital requirements makes it harder for corporations to borrow, by increasing the required ratio of assets to loans.

The reason these policies are contractive, is that scarce credit and less money in circulation tend to limit demand and drive down prices.

When monetary policy is contractive, the impact is to slow down both the rate of inflation and the rate of overall growth.

Managing the economy is a balancing act.

Most important, balance is maintained by implementing policy that is *counter-cyclical* to the general condition of the economy overall.

For example, in the period leading up to the 1929 crash, there was an excess of money in circulation, as well as excessive reliance on the use of credit.

Despite unprecedented speculation in the stock market, the Federal Reserve thought raising interest rates might have too great an impact on the underlying economy.

Those concerns delayed action by the Fed, which only began raising rates in 1928.

Hindsight is 20/20. The expansionary boom should have been addressed in 1927, if not before.

The Fed could have
- raised interest rates,
- increased reserve requirements for banks,
- increased capital requirements for corporations, and
- imposed margin requirements on stock trading

Raising interest rates would have increased the cost of credit.

Increasing reserve requirements for banks would have reduced the amount of money available for lending.

Raising capital requirements would have made it harder for corporations to borrow.

Imposing margin requirements on stock trading would have reduced the amount of money that could be borrowed for speculation.

The impact of *counter-cyclical policy* would have been to offset the boom in the business cycle.

But instead the Fed delayed action, and only began raising interest rates in 1928, when the boom was already out of control.

By comparison, Federal Reserve policy in the 1990s and 2000s was even more at odds with what should have been done.

In the late 1990s, Fed chair Alan Greenspan *lowered interest rates*, at a time when inflation and unemployment were both low.

The impact was to fuel overinvestment in telecommunications that spawned the dot.com boom, and brought unprecedented growth in the stock market.

Thereafter, the dot.com and telecom booms collapsed, and brought trillions in losses.

The Fed's *pro-cyclical policy* of expansion was a disaster.

The Fed should have used *counter-cyclical, contractive policy* to offset the boom, instead of adding fuel to the fire.

Appendix Figure 2
Expansive Policy

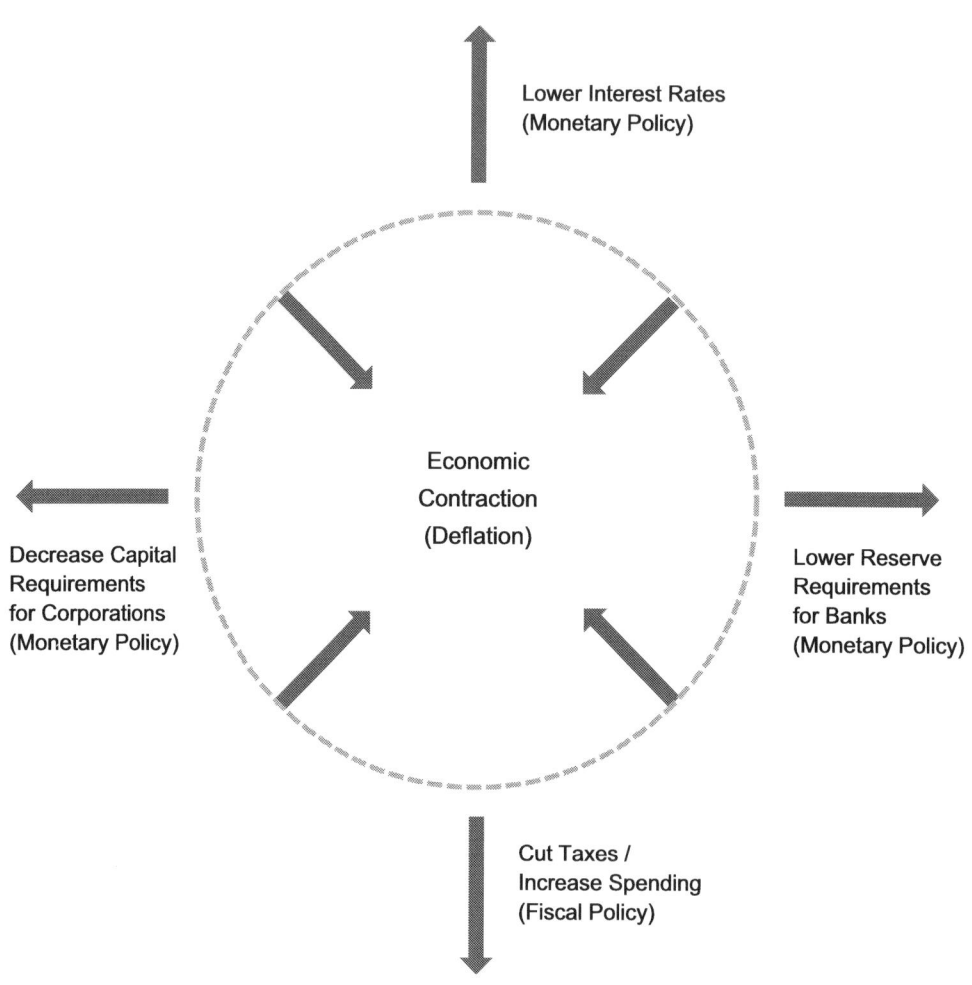

Expansive Policy

At any given point in time, the economy is either shrinking or growing.

When business is slow and sales are down, hiring slows down.

This creates unemployment, which undermines demand, hurts sales even more, and works to shrink the economy.

The impact is deflationary, because the cycle works to decrease the rate of growth in a period of contraction.

When the business cycle is contractive, logic dictates the use of *expansive policy* to offset the downturn in the business cycle.

Such a period of economic contraction is shown in Figure 2, with the economy represented by the area inside the circle.

Arrows pointing inward indicate contraction of the economy.

Arrows outside the circle point outward, and represent *expansive policy tools* used to offset the downturn in the business cycle.

Monetary policy is expansive when interest rates are lowered, and/or
- reserve requirements for banks are lowered,
- capital requirements for corporations are lowered.

Lowering reserve requirements allows banks to set aside less cash in reserve relative to loans.

Lowering capital requirements makes it easier for corporations to borrow, by decreasing the required ratio of assets to loans.

The reason these policies are expansive, is that relaxed credit and more money in circulation tend to stimulate demand and increase growth.

When monetary policy is expansive, the impact is inflationary because the rate of overall growth increases.

For example, the Depression was a period of falling prices (deflation), in which the money supply shrank by one third and the economy contracted by 47 percent.

In 1932 Congress reduced the amount of gold the Fed was required to hold in reserves.

This allowed the Fed to increase the money supply by more than $200 billion in current dollars.

The impact was to prevent any further decline in prices.

By 1932 the Fed had also cut interest rates to less than one percent.

The Fed's monetary policy was counter-cyclical, because expansive policy was implemented at a time when the economy was in a state of contraction.

Even so, the context of 35 percent price declines meant near-zero interest rates had little impact on stimulating investment.

Government taxes and spending, known as fiscal policy, can also be expansive or contractive.

For example, in response to political pressure and signs the economy was beginning to recover, President Roosevelt raised taxes in 1936 and then cut spending in 1937.

The economy declined thereafter, so that by 1938 Roosevelt had become convinced of the validity of using government spending as economic stimulus.

Thereafter, the defense buildup in anticipation of War in Europe then became the basis for large scale spending.

While the war forced the federal government to run huge deficits, the Fed increased the money supply and kept interest rates low.

What ultimately ended the Depression was the combined impact of

- structural reforms designed to support demand (labor standards, social security pensions, and unemployment insurance),
- expansive monetary policy (low interest rates and increased money supply), and
- expansive fiscal policy (increased spending)

The key lesson was that effective policy is counter-cyclical, because expansive policy was implemented at a time when the economy was in a state of contraction.

The economy today is threatened by the onset of deflation.

The cure is expansive policy through public investments needed for growth.

Counter-Cyclical Policy

At any given point in time, the economy is either shrinking or growing.

The lesson of history is simple:

> Counter-cyclical policy is wise;
> Pro-cyclical policy is ill advised.

This dictum is true to the extent that the goal of policy is to maintain balance.

The opposite of balance can be found in periods of economic boom and bust.

For example, when the economy is in a state of contraction, policy that is deflationary serves to reinforce that contraction, and is pro-cyclical.

When President Roosevelt raised taxes in 1936 and then cut spending in 1937, economic decline thereafter served to demonstrate the policy had been pro-cyclical.

In other words, there was not enough growth in the economy to offset Roosevelt's fiscal policies of contraction (higher taxes and less spending).

Managing the economy through counter-cyclical policy is a fundamental principle based on how economies work.

For 60 years after the Great Depression, the use of counter-cyclical policy was not considered to be a partisan issue.

For example, it is ridiculous to argue that expansive policy is liberal, and contractive policy is conservative.

Properly understood, policies of expansion or contraction are neither liberal nor conservative.

But today, opposition to deficit spending has become an ideological position touted by Republicans as a fundamental conservative principle.

Expansive policy like that of the Eisenhower (Republican) administration, is now considered heresy that contradicts conservative principles.

Bruce Bartlett, former chief economist in the Reagan administration, points out how irrational it is to cut spending in the current context of deflation.

When a leading economist in the Reagan administration isn't conservative enough for Congressional Republicans, we should all sit up and take notice.

SWIFT Act proposals are revenue neutral, and rely on elements of both expansive and contractive policy.

For example, SWIFT Act would increase spending on public investments in high technology industries.

However, that increased spending would be funded through financial transaction taxes, as well through tax reform that includes adopting a VAT.

Reader Notes

Reader Notes

Reader Notes

About the Author

I taught political science for five years and received my doctorate from Tulane in 1992. After 20 years in the private sector, my reaction to the Occupy Wall Street movement was to write a series of books and establish the non-profit SWIFT Act Alliance.

The U.S. economy is in crisis, and unprecedented numbers of voters are rejecting the status quo. I wrote these books in the hope of providing a common sense guide to understanding how economies work and why ours no longer functions the way it should.

My goal is to empower readers through explanations that build economic literacy and provide clear discussion of fundamentals that led to the Great Depression and continue today in the Great Recession.

Millions of people realize we can no longer trust the establishment to manage the economy. That means the public will need greater understanding of economic fundamentals to support demands for meaningful reform.

Toward that end, SWIFT Act proposals are intended as a blueprint for what I consider to be essential aspects of reform we need for long term recovery.